The Fall of Athens

Gail Holst-Warhaft

Fomite
Burlington, VT

ISBN-13: 978-1-942515-40-1
Library of Congress Control Number: 2016946768

Fomite
58 Peru Street
Burlington, VT 05401

www.fomitepress.com

Acknowledgements

Translations of Nikos Kavadias's poems are from *The Collected Poems of Nikos Kavadias*, first published by Hakkert (Amsterdam), 1987, reprinted by Cosmos Publishing, 2006. My translation of Kavadias's "To My Horse" was original published in the journal *Aegean*. Translations of Katerina Anghelaki-Rooke's poems appeared in *Modern Poetry in Translation* (UK), and in *The Scattered Papers of Penelope: New and selected poems of Katerina Anghelaki-Rooke*, ed. K. Van Dyck, 2009. Translations of Theodorakis's poetry were originally published in *I Had Three Lives: Selected Poems of Mikis Theodorakis*, Livanis, Athens, 2004, translated by Gail Holst-Warhaft. Translations of other poems set to music by Theodorakis were made at his request and published either in scores or on his website.

For the chapters on Greece and Greek music I refer to books I published years ago including *Road to Rembetika*, Denise Harvey, (original edition1975), and *Theodorakis: Myth and Politics in Modern Greek Music*, (Hakkert, 1980), and to articles published in various journals including *Nation Review* (Australia), and *BookPress* (Ithaca, NY).

Poems on pages 14-30, 174-184, 198, 201, 218, 232-274 are my own. "Wells" and "Grit" were published in *Agenda*, U.K. "Memorials," "Baubo," "Goddess on the Half Shell," "Signor Eulisse in Nafplion" "Bosom", were published in *Per Contra*. "Buried Treasure" was published in the anthology *So Little Time*. "Eurydice" was commissioned by the bass-player Jane Godine and set for soprano and bass. It was performed at the Unitarian Church, Ithaca N.Y. on April 9, 2009.

Books by Gail Holst-Warhaft

Road to Rembetika

Theodorakis: Myth and Politics in Modern Greek Music

Dangerous Voices: Women's Laments and Greek Literature

The Cue for Passion: Grief and its Political Uses

I Had Three Lives: Selected Poems of Mikis Theodorakis

Penelope's Confession

Losing Paradise: The Water Crisis in the Mediterranean (editor)

Contents

Preface: Becoming Elektra   1

1. Letters from Mariza   5
2. The Fall of Athens   14
3. State of Siege   31
4. Exile.   64
5. Return   77
6. Thanassis   94
7. Bouzoukis in Berlin   102
8. Castrato Tenoros, What the Grocer Said, and Some Thoughts on Greek Dancing.   112
9. Zorba   121
10. War, the Sailor and the Mermaid.   136
11. After Life   160
12. Mauthausen   179
13. Great Expectations — the Burden of Philhellenism   192
14. Eros and Katerina   210
15. Greeks, Old and New   226
16. Aristophanes in a Basement   233
17. Aristophanes at Epidaurus   246
18. Once in a Lifetime   269
Epilogue   273

Preface: Becoming Elektra

Perhaps it was because I wasn't Greek that Mariza began to tell me her story. Or perhaps it was because I listened. Among the *kallitechnes*, the artists of Athens, everyone had a story. The years of the German Occupation, the Civil War that followed, the persecution of the Left by the victorious right-wing forces, and the Military Dictatorship of 1967-74 had disproportionally affected them. Most artists and intellectuals had supported the Left. They had faced danger, prison, torture. Theirs were moral tales, tales of heroism. Mariza's was a story without a moral. It was about poverty and what it drove her mother to do, about what it takes to become a famous artist when you begin with less than nothing. Like most people's stories, it could be told again and again and each time it would be a different story. Some of it was fact and some she had to invent. Like the part about her father. What did she know about Willy Koch, the German officer her mother loved and had two children by before he disappeared? How and why did Mariza take his name when she was twenty years old? Why did no-one ask where she got a name that was not Greek?

Mariza's story deserves a book to itself. Enough to say that Mariza is my closest Greek friend, my lifeline to the music, the politics, the sadness and the beauty of Greece. Ever since we met in the 1970's, she has been talking and singing to me. Because she is from the island of Santorini, I've learned the songs of the Aegean islands, the sayings of the villages, the words for poor people's food and for weeds you can eat. I've also read the poets she set to music.

For Mariza, I am Elektra, a name I adopted during a winter I spent on the island of Aigina. My neighbors had complained about my name; how could I be so Greek and have a funny name they found difficult to pronounce? "Why don't you choose a Greek name?" one of them asked, and without a moment's thought I said "Elektra." Say what you like about symbolism, I chose it for the sound of those three bunched consonants that are pronounced so richly in Greek that they sound like biting into dark chocolate.

From then on I was Elektra to Greeks who were not comfortable with English. Mariza and I used to communicate by telephone, but over these last years of economic catastrophe in Greece, when phone calls to and from Greece became too expensive, she began sending emails to me. Mariza, who hardly went to school and had no interest in whatever was taught there, is able to express herself more eloquently than most people I know. Perhaps the fact that she knows thousands of songs and poems by heart has been the perfect education for a singer and song-writer who was once as famous as any artist in Greece and who now teaches children to sing their own language.

This book is about a country and a city I came to love. I sometimes think of Greece as an aging lover, his beard turned grey, a glint still in his eye. We sit in a square under a plane tree and share half a kilo of wine. "Still paradise, eh?" he asks. "Mmmm," I say, inhaling the intoxicating fumes of gasoline, fried fish and orange blossom. There are beggars on every corner, nobody knows where their next euro is coming from, empty houses and apartments are everywhere, but this is still Greece. Since it became a country, it has been small, poor and beleaguered, and people have still sat in the squares drinking wine. By the second glass we begin to sing, my old Greek lover and I. We sing a song every Greek knows. It's by Vassilis Tsitsanis.

To listen to the song, visit goo.gl/QHOAQq

Συννεφιασμένη Κυριακή

Συννεφιασμένη Κυριακή,
μοιάζεις με την καρδιά μου
που έχει πάντα συννεφιά,
Χριστέ και Παναγιά μου.

Cloudy Sunday

Cloudy Sunday
you're like my heart
that's always cloudy.
Christ and the Virgin!

Είσαι μια μέρα σαν κι αυτή,
που 'χασα την χαρά μου.
συννεφιασμένη Κυριακή,
ματώνεις την καρδιά μου.

You're a day like the one
when I lost my joy;
cloudy Sunday
you make my heart bleed.

Όταν σε βλέπω βροχερή,
στιγμή δεν ησυχάζω.
Μαύρη μου κάνεις τη ζωή,
και βαριαναστενάζω.

When I see you rainy
I can't find peace.
You make my life black
and I sigh deeply.

"Remember," says my aging Greek, "that song was written during the German Occupation. Our songs were about remembering, not forgetting. Someone will remember this present misery too, and we'll all sing about it until the sky clears."

So, with the help of my Greek friends, I have tried to write my own song about remembering. It is dedicated to Mikis Theodorakis, Mariza Koch, Katerina Anghelaki-Rooke, Thanassis Athanassiou, Dionysis Savvopoulos, Iakovos Kambanellis, and the many other friends who taught me how to sing in Greek.

My thanks, as always, to my friends in poetry and my most careful readers, first among them, my sadly lamented and dear friend Jon Stallworthy, who had enough time to read these poems before he died. Thanks to my husband Zellman, to David Curzon, Chana Kronfeld, and the Ithaca poets I meet with regularly to exchange poems: Laura Glenn, Jack Hopper, Peter Fortunato, and Cory Brown. A special thanks to Greg Delanty, who suggested Fomite Press look at my poems, and to Marc Estrin and Donna Bister who turned what I thought was a collection of poems into an eclectic book that surprised me as much as I hope it will surprise the reader.

1. Letters from Mariza

October 2013

Elektra, you've left me here in Athens and I don't have anyone to tell the things that come out of my head to. It's not even two months since you left, but if you were to arrive now, you'd find the same Athens you discovered before the dictatorship. We all look each other in the eye, we communicate with one another, we curse the thieves of politicians from head to toe without being afraid of the secret files of the sixties. I don't know where they've hidden the *lafiria* (do you know the word? If it's not in the dictionary it must go into it urgently! Otherwise it would take a sheet of A4 paper to explain to you exactly what it means*).

Autumn's here and people with the doors of their houses open are drinking their wine with friends. The tavernas have emptied but there were an awful lot of them, you have to admit…. The Germans are wise to envy us. They don't need the sun that makes you sit on the verandah with your mouth open, because their language doesn't have a lot of vowels — it's all consonants. They're condemned to speak through their teeth. We've found a way to make the bitter, sweet. We're all going around without a penny in our pockets and if you followed ten people around Syntagma Square, you'd be lucky to find six euros dropped on the ground.

On Santorini we say the stomach doesn't have windows. That's why we still hide our wretchedness with dignity. When we're finally walking around in rags 'the herrings will weep for us in their boxes, and the babies in their swaddling-clothes.'

It is critical moment – in the sense of a useful one – and the feeling we all have is that we must be united. Whatever happens is for the good of Greece— that's what we all feel. When you phone me I'll remind you of the story I told you, the one all Greeks know, about a war that will begin in 2012 starting in Syria. The war will be over water and the Muscovites will come down and snatch the tassel from the red fez; as Saint Paiisios writes 'those with the fez have funeral wheat in their pockets.'

I'm trying to tell you it in a cheerful way, not a demagogic way. Here's what they say. About 1780, before the Turks destroyed Epirus, Saint Kosmas the Aetolian said "Greece will be free when the head of Ali Pasha goes to Constantinople. In the years to come there will be three world wars. The third will be caused by the drying up of the Tigris and Euphrates. The barbarity of this war will be unlike anything the world has ever seen. The Turkish calf will swim in blood because the white bear from the north will attack him. The Russians will come down to the Aegean and the Russian Patriarch, in his white robe, will conduct the liturgy in Saint Sophia."

I write you this with the fingers of Dina, who is smiling and says she has known this story since she was a child.

Saint Kosmas said that the war will be over religion and water, and that Greece will be allied with Russia. Here, we have the sense that it has begun already, something like a prophecy.

November

My Elektra, good morning and a good week to you! Here in the homeland we have a Prime Minister again. As much as we can, we tighten our belts. We never even dreamed, in those sunny summer days, that the time would come when the coffee we drank would be half coffee and half barley. We don't have anything to chew, but the cauldron's boiling.

I'm happy because I've made you dizzy with all this!

February

It's Saturday. I woke at seven to the sound of shouting. I went up to the terrace and saw that the whole Acropolis was covered with demonstrators holding an enormous banner. You can guess the words. I grabbed a red tablecloth from downstairs and gave them a signal. They answered back, full of enthusiasm to see they had a supporter. Then I had to go down to the basement because I had a class.

Every Saturday I have fifty-seven children. I'm still here and I don't know what's going on in the outside world but you know that everything is hanging by a thread. Our poor country! I don't want to give you a picture of Athens because I know you love it so much. Our young people are sleeping on benches in this cold. 250 servings of food a day don't cover the needs of the homeless.

I feel we'll survive because we were born to create unexpected things. Money doesn't circulate here and anyone who knows how to cook takes care of the others; the old Greek hospitality has come back. What we call solidarity. We live.

March.

Elektra, Look! Something beautiful for you. The first day of spring and Poetry Day. I just got back from Syntagma Square, at the fountain where Greek poets are marching to demonstrate their indignation about what's happening.

I carried a banner too. The slogans had lines of poetry by the greatest poets. It was such a perfect, sunny day with drums and people walking on stilts. I talked to young people who sleep in the square on benches at night or in improvised tents. They take turns sleeping and watching over each other in case they get robbed.

May 4

Dear Elektra,

We have summer here – what about you?

We have other things too. We have elections. As a writer you could have described this historic moment in Greece through your own filter. You could have given a picture of the wretched homeless. Of the thousands of "for sale" and "for rent" signs all over the city, and in the posh suburbs, empty villas with swimming pools and security alarms. The question you'd have to ask is, since the greedy rich who are scared stiff have left their houses to save their skins, where are they living? Maybe there are catacombs somewhere in Greece and we don't know about it and only *they* have the keys to them? Or maybe they've escaped and scattered to countries all over the world?

Here in the house things are as you know them. Leica was 'engaged,' but she'll probably marry in September because the bridegroom's owner didn't want to leave her dog here for a few days. Liveloula has discovered the next-door terrace, which has become a garden and she's fascinated. She brings me all the crickets she catches there. Manolis and Christina have started thinking about moving to Canada with Anatoli. Manolis' half-brother lives there. Has he forgotten what it means to be over fifty? I can't stop them, despite the fact that I've become their cook with all those Tupperware containers I fill every day, and not only for them, but for other people I love in the neighborhood. But they can't solve their economic problems here so they have to think of something. Maybe they'll go to France and I'll lose my only grandchild.

I hear people say that in Europe, where lots of young Greeks have fled, they've created communities and the sort of solidarity they had during the dictatorship…you remember the song "No one here sings, no-one dances…"

Last night the speech of the old leftist Manolis Glezos in Omonia Square was moving. He'll be 90 next year. The square was full. I don't know where they'd hidden the homeless and the foreigners. The rally had a pulse to it.

May God lend a hand! If I tell you about the danger of the fascists from the 'Golden Dawn' Party getting into parliament I'll make you sad.

What can I write for you to make you a little happy? I went to Nafplion before the 1st of May and among the thousands of poppies that I looked at very carefully one by one – something I do every year, because the poppy is my favorite flower – I found one plant by itself with four blossoms, and between the red and the black there was a tiny white stripe. I tied a red ribbon around the stem in case I could find it again when it finished flowering and take the seed to Kardamyli. We'll see. I'm sending you pictures of it.

May 15th

Elektra, what a lovely surprise your phone-call was yesterday. I was in the courtyard with Leica who keeps whining all the time because I don't take her for a walk. The reason is if I leave the house and go as far as the next corner, I get mixed up in ten conversations. So I sit in my cage and wither because of everything that's happening in my beloved country.

The other day I noticed something strange. Instead of going white, my hair's going black. Probably because I'm cooped up so much. So I telephoned a hairdresser and she came and put highlights in my hair, because I had a concert that was being videotaped and there's no way I can start changing my image now. Once I used to say that before I turned 70 I'd have stopped singing, and I'd be free to wander along the beaches. So I had enough patience to be deprived of nature for a while. Now that hope's gone and I'll have to go on singing beyond the age of 70, I'm thinking about becoming a nun in a beautiful seaside nunnery in the Peloponnese. I've never been inside, but I want to go and see what sort of creature the abbess is. If I find her charming you've lost me.

January 20ᵗʰ 2015

Good morning Elektra, from sunny Athens.

As you know, these pre-election days, Athens is a madhouse with wings. You can't imagine what we hear. The candidates promise us the moon and the stars. The Europeans threaten us with a new crisis, and they don't understand that a person who's soaked to the skin isn't afraid of the rain. I always used to have confidence in the imponderable factors the Greeks created during the centuries, and the fact that we somehow slid out of the worst predictions of our enemies; now I'm afraid the neo-colonialists have digitized our resistance.

Still, I keep hoping. Remember the lines from the poem "The Sovereign Sun," by Elytis:

Όμορφη και παράξενη πατρίδα
    Ωσάν αυτή που μου 'λαχε δεν είδα'

Ρίχνει να πιάσει ψάρια   πιάνει φτερωτά
    Στήνει στη γη καράβι   κήπο στα νερά

Κλαίει φιλεί το χώμα   ξενιτεύεται
    Μένει στους πέντε δρόμους   αντρειεύεται

Κάνει να πάρει πέτρα   τηνε παρατά
    Κάνει να τη σκαλίσει   βγάνει θάματα

Μπαίνει σ' ένα βαρκάκι   πιάνει ωκεανούς
    Ξεσηκωμούς γυρεύει   θέλει τύραννους

Πέντε μεγάλους βγάνει   πάνω τους βαρεί
    Να λείψουν απ' τη μέση   τους δοξολογεί.

Mariza Koch

Beautiful, strange homeland. I'll never see
a country like the one fate gave me.

It tries to catch some fish catches birds instead
builds a boat on land at sea a garden bed.

Weeps, kisses the earth goes away again.
Stays on five roads becomes a man.

Goes to pick up a stone leaves it there.
Digs the ground finds miracles to disinter.

Aboard a little boat sails the seven seas.
Goes to find uprisings seeks tyrants to appease.

Produces five great men then starts a fight;
sings their praises when they're out of sight.

All the mountains of Greece are white with snow from the terrible weather we've had the last weeks. And today I woke up with the sun shining brightly, the fireplaces damped, the temperature has reached 18c and the squares are full of people sitting in the sun. The bitter oranges are shining like Christmas trees and something that you'll notice when you come, *me to kalo*: the cafes have multiplied by ten. If all this was happening and there was proper education and culture, I wouldn't be afraid of anything.

Sadly, though, the teachers have grown into frightened little people because they come from the post-dictatorship generation of populism, of stadiums and the affluence that went with it. This crisis we're living through will produce Greeks who are more aware, who are better people. I see it in the eyes of the adolescents.

March, 2015

My Elektra,

Monday today and rain and cold all over Greece. As they say " Save some wood for March so you don't burn the orchard stakes."

Yesterday I went to look at the theater in Faleron where I'll be singing in a big children's concert in May. In the courtyard there are some kiosks where the homeless have taken shelter. They never leave because there's a children's play-center nearby and they come out to beg there. The guard of the theater knows them and says the mayor sends them a serving of hot food each day.

When I went they were all out, but under each blanket was a cat. It was their protector and their heating for the night. A strange commune for about ten people adrift in life. But it smelled of alcohol and hopelessness.

I'm sorry if I've made you sad.

I'm wearing an overcoat because it's cold in the house and there's no heating oil left. Besides clothes, God gives the cold. He sees we still have warm clothes, so he gives us as much cold as we can bear.

This afternoon I'll pick up Liveloula from the veterinary hospital. They did some tests for a lump that appeared on her back and the results weren't good. Luckily she's not in pain. What can we do? We'll bring her home and for as long as she lasts, she'll enjoy our love. God also made the difficult things.

I want to send you something beautiful. Yesterday I took a picture of an almond tree in blossom. It was as if it were singing the song of spring. Please stay with this picture because I've saddened you a lot.

Almond Tree

2. The Fall of Athens

City

There's a city I arrived at young and made
my own. No city will take its place.
I walked its worn streets past shops
where printing presses clattered, chalices
censers, candlesticks, amulets were hammered,
shops sold pastries, sheet-music,
canaries, olives, bridal dresses
of white meringue, lottery tickets.

From basement taverns, thick with oil
and smoke, came bitter love songs
and cats leapt from roof to roof.
At noon I sat under a mulberry-tree
sipping wine in a whitewashed square.
Above, stood the ruins of a city
heavy with history where tourists swarmed.
All I wanted was here, in this square.

When I returned a bank stood
on the street of sandal-makers, the organ grinder
and his creaking songs had disappeared.
I walked streets with familiar names
where photographs faded in empty rooms
and for rent, for rent, read paper signs
angled on peeling plaster walls
and I was a stranger in the city I loved.

2013 C.E.

Her brother died in June,
a holiday week-end

and no funeral parlor
to take the body away.

Heat wrapped the city
in a shroud of brown gauze;

half the apartments in Athens
dark, power cut off,

bills unpaid. She remembered
when tin beds were dragged

into the streets, to catch
the pre-dawn breeze.

Men in striped pajama
bottoms and singlets chatted,

smoked Asos unfiltered;
now none would dare.

On morning TV his sister
blames the undertakers, the church,

the government. His final days
took their savings, her jewels;

now no-one will take the body.
In the scandal-weary city

the story still shocks.
An undertaker offers to store

the corpse till the funeral day
but she fails to navigate

the sea of papers required
to bury the dead in time.

The undertaker regrets his gesture;
the sister will pay with interest

for voicing despair. Only
the dead are patient here.

(after Thucydides, II.49)

In *the summer of 430 BC*
when Archidamus attacked, plague

entered the city like poison
gas, beginning in Piraeus.

First headaches, then sneezing,
vomiting, an inner burning

that made the lightest linen
scorch like Medea's gift.

Strangest how the birds scorned
corpses and the sky emptied.

Even dogs refused
till hunger made them mad.

Some buried the dead as best
they could. Unable to pay

for a pyre they heaped their dead
on fires meant for others.

Laments not sung; the dead
were left unwept, unburied.

2013

In the rich suburbs swimming-pools
were *de rigueur* among the rich

yet when the ailing state tried
to collect a tax on them

they were suddenly rare as
ivory-billed woodpeckers.

From the air officials saw
a thousand blue eyes staring.

Comeuppance seemed close
till a rush on green tarpaulins

turned water into grass,
stymying satellite and state.

(after Thucydides, II.53)

"As for what is called honor
none obeyed its laws."

Why fear the anger of men
or gods when good and bad

died the same death
and few survived to be punished?

Since life was cheap they spent
all their money on luxuries.

Beyond the city the enemy
laid waste the land.

People remembered an oracle
that said the Dorians would come

and plague with them but some
argued over the meaning of it,

calling it famine, a tightening
of belts, not certain death.

News Report, 2012.

On the sidewalk near Omonia Station
a man lies shivering in a sleeping bag.
"I'm eighty-two," he tells a reporter.
"Feels like I'm in my grave already."

Surely he has a relative here
or in some dying mountain village?
Maybe he fought with his family and thought
his pension would last him out.

Not since the winter of forty-two
when carts collected the daily dead
has Athens seen such sights.
These Greeks are new at homelessness.

(after Aristophanes' Acharnians, 425BCE)

We old veterans have a bone to pick
with the city of Athens. It's a scandal that we
who fought great sea-battles for you
are left high and dry in old age.
We're cast aside and destitute – worse,
we're dragged into court, badgered by lawyers
for a fat fee. Old codgers now
we squeak like an aulos with a broken reed.

We lean on our sticks stammering like toddlers,
wrapped in a fog of legalese. Even Tithonus
is a tongue-tied fool. Forced to pay
for his defeat he staggers off in tears
and tells his friends what he'd saved
for a coffin has been consumed in fees.

October, 2013

She was caught traveling on an Athens bus
without a ticket and couldn't pay
the seventy-two-Euro fine.

If you fail to pay a fine it grows
like a virus, like weeds, the sorrows of Job.
After twenty days it multiplies ten-fold,

a sum she can't imagine in her dreams.
Unemployed, living with her disabled mother,
behind with rent like half her generation,

no health insurance, she expects no mercy
from a state wrung dry by its own greed
and the demands of its creditors,

northerners who never strayed from the path,
who paid their debts, saved for their future
to enjoy, one summer, the ruin of Greeks.

(after Plutarch, *Life of Solon*)

Solon's laws were passed to avoid
a debt crisis – he decreed a seisachtheia
a shaking off of burdens… seismograph
contains the shaking, with achthos,
a weight, also a grievance. Before Solon
debtors could be enslaved having used
their bodies as collateral. Others were forced
into exile and forgot their own tongue.
Some said debts were not cancelled
under his laws, only interest lowered.
In any case, he boasted he had lifted
the mortgage stones from Athens,
setting its people free.

2012-2014

In myth everything was possible – matricide, self-mutilation,
children served up to their father for dinner, bodies torn
apart by dogs or crazed women, husbands murdered
in the bath. Dramas were set in the distant past, horrors
kept off stage. Myths were warnings of what might happen
if grief got loose, if each death was answered by another.

In Greece these days the grief-crazed climb to the terrace.
They hold hands. Perhaps they kiss for a last time.
Then they jump. They don't expect a god to intervene.
If he hasn't already, as their lives diminished day by day,
there's little chance he'll open a parachute above their heads
before the hot concrete rises to meet them.

A cell phone calls, an ambulance collects the fallen:
a son and the senile mother he can't afford to keep,
a bankrupt father with an infant under each arm.
No monument marks the spot. They fell not in war,
not for their country, because of it. In Greece these days
It's hard to keep the horror off stage.

Fall

My father was a nifty man,
could fix an axle, fashion
a maze for Midas' offspring;
why not trust his wings?

Don't worry about the heat
of the sun he told me, the coat
of wax I used is thick
enough. Only a lunatic

or a dutiful son would take
his word, but I'd seen him create
machines that told the time
and such a perfect system

for draining the palace water
that my faith didn't falter.
He strapped them carefully on
and led me to the megaron.

We climbed to the roof-edge
and I waited, wax-fledged,
for the wind to carry me
soaring like an eagle, effortlessly,

to the chariot Helios drives
each day across the sky.
And suddenly I was lifted up
into the terrible blue lap

of the gods, an odorless aether.
Freed of every earthly fetter,
I unstrapped my harness, preferring
death on earth to wings.

3. State of Siege

June 1, 1967. Army Order No. 13
It is decided and so ordered that throughout the country it is forbidden to reproduce or play the music and songs of the composer Mikis Theodorakis, the former leader of the now disbanded "Lambrakis Youth" because this music is in the service of communism;
To sing any songs used by the communist youth movement which was dissolved under Paragraph 8 of the Decree of May 6, 1967 since these songs arouse passions and cause strife among the people; Citizens who contravene this Order will be immediately brought before the military tribunal and judged under martial law.
General Odysseas Angelis

April 21st, 1967

At 3 a.m. Mikis Theodorakis is woken by a phone call. He has been at a club in Kolonaki, listening to his new singer, Maria Farandouri, perform his latest cycle of songs. They are settings of the poetry of Federico Garcia Lorca, sung in Elytis's splendid Greek translation. The composer is excited by his songs and still under Lorca's spell. He leaves the club for his home at midnight, and works for an hour or more before falling asleep. The phone-call is from a friend who has heard there are tanks rolling through Constitution Square and stopping in front of the Greek Parliament. Theodorakis tries to call his left wing friends. The lines are dead. He wakes his wife, Myrto.

She is used to such crises. Immediately alert, she tells him to dress. She will burn any incriminating papers but he must flee the house.

"Should we wake the children?" he asks.

"No, let them sleep," she answers. "It will only upset them."

He kisses her quickly and slips out into the street.

*   *   *

Even if he were not famous, at six feet four inches with a mop of curly hair that adds another inch or two to his height, Theodorakis is a conspicuous figure in any Greek crowd; he finds the street outside his home deserted and runs to a colleague's house. He wakes his friend and tells him to warn anyone in the Movement. He telephones home. Myrto has only time to whisper "They're here!" before she hangs up.

At his friend's house, the radio is playing military marches. A voice interrupts the music to declare a 'State of Siege'. Theodorakis and the few members of the Lambrakis Youth Movement who have escaped the drag-net gather at the house where he is hiding to plan a strategy for resistance. The net begins to close around the neighborhood of Nea Smyrni, a sub-urb settled by refugees from Asia Minor that has always been sympathetic to the Left. Patrols are on every corner. The composer knows he must escape the area fast. He makes a false moustache of cotton wool dipped in black varnish and creeps from garden to garden to reach a safe house where he is picked up and driven away. Somehow the car gets through the police blockades and reaches a safer neighborhood. The tall man with the false moustache is smuggled into another friendly house to hide.

*   *   *

By the time the sun rises on the pristine spring morning of April 21st, 1967, thousands of people have been arrested in the major towns of Greece. In Athens, the jails are overflowing and the remaining prisoners are herded into the hippodrome. The police already have lists of all the real and suspected leftists in the country. Since the leftist forces, led by the Communist Party, lost the Civil War of 1947-49, suspected Communists have been hounded, imprisoned, exiled, tortured and murdered. Only for the last few years have they had any representation in the Greek parliament and a voice in Greece's cultural life, but they have never felt safe. Only four years earlier, Grigoris Lambrakis was murdered. Anyone who has seen the Costa-Gavras movie *Z* will remember the charismatic doctor and parliamentarian played by Yves Montand, who was hit by a three-wheeled vehicle as he crossed the street in Salonika on his way to speak at a political rally. The two men in the vehicle dragged him inside and beat him over the head before they threw him back into the street. That night he died of brain injuries in the hospital. Lambrakis's murder set off a chain of events that led indirectly to the coup d'état.

Like Lambrakis, Theodorakis was a representative of the United Left Party in the Greek Parliament, and the two men were friends. When he heard of the attack on Lambrakis, he flew from Athens to Salonika. Thousands were gathered outside the hospital waiting for news. Lambrakis was not just a politician. He was a star – a handsome Olympic athlete and a professor of Medicine. After a trip to England, where he had been impressed by the "Ban the Bomb" movement and the marches Bertrand Russell and others organized to oppose nuclear weapons, he formed his own peace movement in Greece. The marches he organized followed the legendary route Pheidipides ran from Marathon to Athens. On the first march, police arrested and beat the marchers until only Lambrakis was left. His parliamentary immunity protected him for the time being, but he was a marked man. There was no doubt in the minds of the people outside the Salonika hospital that the attack on Lambrakis was politically motivated.

Theodorakis and other colleagues of the slain deputy accompanied the body of Lambrakis back to Athens. The atmosphere at the funeral was explosive. Scuffles broke out and a student was shot by the police. Theodorakis was outraged by the death of his friend and the intimidation of the students, and he formed a youth movement in Lambrakis's

Μάρτυρες ήρωες οδηγούνε
τα γαλάζια μάτια του μάς καλούνε

Sotiri Petroula, Sotiri Petroula,
nightingale and lion, mountain and clear sky
nightingale and lion, mountain and clear sky
Martyrs, heroes lead us;
his blue eyes call us.

Σωτήρη Πέτρουλα, Σωτήρη Πέτρουλα
οδήγα το λαό σου οδήγα μας μπροστά
οδήγα το λαό σου οδήγα μας μπροστά
Μάρτυρες ήρωες οδηγούνε
τα γαλάζια μάτια του μάς καλούνε

Sotiri Petroula, Sotiri Petroula,
lead your people, lead us forward.
Martyrs, heroes lead us;
his blue eyes call us.

The song became the anthem for a movement.

*   *   *

Sotiris Petroulas

A country that bans not just political songs, but everything a composer has written must, I realized, believe deeply in the power of music. It also believed in poetry. Greece in the 1960's had more poetry publishers and poetry bookshops than any country in Europe. Two of its poets, George Seferis and Odysseas Elytis, won the Nobel

Prize for Literature in the 1960's and 70's. One of the most influential poets of the twentieth century was Constantine Cavafy. Yiannis Ritsos's poems have been translated into every major European language.

In 1959, when there had been some easing of the persecution of the Greek Left, and Yannis Ritsos's poems were published, he sent a cycle called *Epitaphios* to Paris, where Mikis Theodorakis was studying and composing. The composer and his wife Myrto had both traveled to Paris in 1954 on scholarships, she to study radiology at the Curie Institute, he to study composition under Olivier Messiaen at the Paris conservatory. By then Theodorakis had been imprisoned and tortured several times. Greek political life was dangerous for anyone known to be sympathetic to the Left, and Paris was full of young Greeks escaping persecution. Yiannis Xenakis and Theodorakis were among them.

The arrival of two children soon put an end to Myrto's scientific career, but Mikis was already a promising classical composer, with a ballet (*Antigone*) commissioned by Sadler's Wells, a dozen symphonic works, and several film scores behind him. Yiannis Ritsos was older than Theodorakis and already a famous poet when the young composer began writing music. Theodorakis admired him greatly and shared his political beliefs. Reading the revised poem *Epitaphios* that Ritsos sent him in Paris changed his life. While Myrto shopped for groceries at a Paris store, he sat outside in the car feverishly scribbling melodies in the margins of the poems. By morning he had written a whole cycle of songs.

The Greece Theodorakis had left behind was in ferment. His colleagues were risking their lives to demonstrate, to protest, to encourage the remnants of the demoralized Left, defeated in the Civil War and imprisoned for a decade following it, to take an active role in every sphere of Greek life. As he penciled melodies for Ritsos's *Epitaphios* beside the text, Theodorakis did what Ritsos no doubt intended him to do: he decided that he could not stay in Paris writing esoteric modern music for a sophisticated audience. He would return to Greece, record his new

"Do you know who that is?"

"No."

"It's Grigoris Bithikotsis. He's a singer. He's written some good songs too. He's doing his military service, but he'll make a lot of money in the bouzouki clubs when he gets out."

The name and the gesture had remained with Theodorakis through the horrors of torture, thirst and starvation in the Makronissos concentration camp. Now, after years of studying, writing and performing nothing but classical music, they surfaced. Theodorakis sent out word that he wanted to hear Grigoris Bithikotsis sing. Despite the fact that Ritsos's lyrics were spoken in a mother's voice, the young singer's voice was exactly what Theodorakis was looking for. For years he had shared pain and hunger with men like Bithikotsis. He wanted to reach out to them, to the masses of ordinary Greeks who had suffered under the Metaxas Dictatorship in the 1930's, under the German Occupation, during the brutal Civil War, and the persecution of the Left that followed. He was, many thought, naïve. He believed that his music, combined with the poetry of his country's best poets, could change Greece.

In the summer of 1960, Theodorakis's recording of *Epitaphios* was released almost simultaneously with Manos Hadzidakis's. Hadzidakis had chosen the young singer Nana Mouskouri to record his arrangements. The Bithikotsis recording became an overnight success that soon eclipsed Hadzidakis's version. It also caused, as Hadzidakis had predicted, a furor among Greek intellectuals. Theodorakis was criticized for his attempt to combine sophisticated poetry with rembetika-style music, especially with the bouzouki. Left wing intellectuals pointed out that the rembetika were decadent songs filled with references to drugs and prison life. They were completely inappropriate to combine with the poetry of Ritsos. But working-class Greeks saw no conflict. They heard a voice they loved singing powerful songs, and they responded. They were familiar with the imagery of Ritsos's songs, much of it taken from the folk tradition. For them there was no such thing as "high" or "low" art. Poetry and song were simply there, like water, like hunger. A necessary part of their lives.

A protest organized in Salonika in 1936 by striking tobacco workers for better conditions, had been savagely put down by the police. A newspaper photograph had captured a mother bending over her son's body, lying where he had been shot by the police, on the street. The picture inspired Yiannis Ritsos to compose a series of poems in the voice of the mother, a *mater dolorosa* who reminded him of the most solemn moment of the Greek Orthodox Church litany – the *Epitaphios* service on Good Friday, when the dead Christ is mourned not only by his mother but by the women of the congregation who spend the day decorating his bier with flowers.

In the song "A Day in May," the mother remembers how her dead son used to stand on the flat roof of their house looking at the stars:

Μέρα Μαγιού μου μίσεψες, μέρα Μαγιού σε χάνω
άνοιξη γιε που αγάπαγες κι ανέβαινες απάνω

A day in May you left me, a day in May I lose you,
in spring my son, when you loved to go up

Στο λιακωτό και κοίταζες και δίχως να χορταίνεις
άρμεγες με τα μάτια σου το φως της οικουμένης.

to the terrace and look up and never tiring of it
you'd milk the light of the universe with your eyes.

To hear the song, visit goo.gl/t8APVp

The verb "milk," sublime and homely, tied the mother and her son to the humblest of rural activities while they gazed, rapt, at the wonder of the stars. It wasn't only the poetry that made the hairs on your arms stand on end. It had to do with the way the words were set to music and performed. The song was in the rhythm of a *zeibekiko*, the only solo dance in the Greek repertoire, a dance I had watched on many nights since I had arrived in Athens. A bouzouki-player would pick out a tune, or a man would put a coin in a juke-box, and a song would begin in a curious, exciting meter. Arms stretched to the sides like a bird in flight, a cigarette dangling from his lip, the dancer would begin to walk unsteadily in a circle that spiraled inwards. No two dancers performed the dance in the same way. Some would lurch and sway, occasionally dropping to their knees. Others would leap and slap their shoes with one hand. The only constraints were the inward turn of the dancer, the outflung arms, and the casual body posture that belied the dancer's intense concentration.

In Theodorakis's song, the masculine drama of the dance was accentuated by the voice of Bithikotsis. It had a flat, slightly nasal quality that I had heard in the music of the Orthodox Church. It had no vibrato. Its power came from a total security of tone, placement and timing that gave off a whiff of unmistakable male pride tempered by restraint. People who have known oppression learn to disguise pride. I had heard the same restrained dignity in the voices of gypsy musicians from Spain, and of black American jazz musicians. In each case the surface control seemed effortless, accentuating the power that lay beneath, like skin stretched over a drum-head. But how could such a voice represent a mother lamenting her son?

It would take time to recognize that Bithikotsis's voice, and the sharp sonority of the bouzouki were not incongruous with a mother's lament for her murdered son; on the contrary, they seemed perfectly appropriate. Ritsos's lamenting mother was an archetype of the Greek mother, especially the mother of a son on wrong side of the political and economic divide.

Mikis Theodorakis, Manos Hadzidakis and Nana Mouskouri, who recorded Hadzidakis's setting of the Epitaphios cycle in September 1960.

To hear the album, **Epitaphios** visit goo.gl/lL67X1

Three Sections of Ritsos's Epitaphios set to music by Theodorakis.

Πού πέταξε τ' αγόρι μου

Γιε μου, σπλάχνο των σπλάχνων μου, καρδούλα της καρδιάς μου
πουλάκι της φτωχιάς αυλής, ανθέ της ερημιάς μου.

Πού πέταξε τ' αγόρι μου, πού πήγε, πού μ' αφήνει;
Χωρίς πουλάκι το κλουβί, χωρίς νερό η κρήνη.

Πώς κλείσαν τα ματάκια σου και δεν θωρείς που κλαίω
και δεν σαλεύεις δεν γροικάς τα που πικρά σου λέω.

Πού πέταξε τ' αγόρι μου, πού πήγε, πού μ' αφήνει;
Χωρίς πουλάκι το κλουβί, χωρίς νερό η κρήνη.

Where Did My Bird Fly?

My son, flesh of my flesh, dear heart of my heart,
little bird of the poor courtyard, flower of my desert.

Where did my bird fly? Where did he go? How could he leave me?
Cage with no bird, spring with no water.

How could your eyes be closed and not see me weep?
And you don't stir, don't hear my bitter words.

Where did my bird fly? Where did he go? How did he leave me?
Cage with no bird, spring with no water.

The Sun and Time (1967)

*On the fourth floor at Bouboulinas Street prison, cell number 4, I waited
for torture and death. On the fourth of September they brought me pa-
per and pencil. Then I wrote 32 poems. I had spent the previous nights
sleepless, with my back pressed to the wall, waiting from moment to mo-
ment for them to take me for torture or execution. My whole existence
was marked by the expectation of certain death. As time flowed patiently
by and I suffered, I saw clearly in my head the image of the final moment.
The morning sky was a deep blue. The air was transparent, crystal clear.
What would I call out at this final moment? This thought tormented me...
This torment was followed by an inexplicable euphoria. I was happy! In
the end death isn't so terrible. Perhaps it's beautiful, I say to the guard...
I'm not a poet, but when the verses began to hammer at my brain I felt
how words could be dressed in blood. How they could liberate me. I am an
artist. I defeat time and death...*

I am Time.

(from Mikis Theodorakis To Chreos- The Debt, II)

Selections from the album can be heard at goo.gl/HQ8dfu

iv

Ἐπάνω στὸ ξερὸ χῶμα τῆς καρδιᾶς μου
ξεφύτρωσε ἕνας κάκτος

πέρασαν πάνω ἀπό εἴκοσι αἰώνες
ποὺ ὀνειρεύομαι γιασεμί
τὰ μαλλιά μου μύρισαν γιασεμί
ἡ φωνή μου εἶχε πάρει κάτι
ἀπό τὸ λεπτὸ ἄρωμά του
τὰ ροῦχα μου μύρισαν γιασεμί
ἡ ζωή μου εἶχε πάρει κάτι
ἀπό τὸ λεπτὸ ἄρωμά του

ὅμως ὁ κάκτος δὲν εἶναι κακός
μονάχα δὲν τὸ ξέρει καὶ φοβᾶται

κοιτάζω τὸν κάκτο μελαγχολικά
πότε πέρασαν κιόλας τόσοι αἰώνες

θὰ ζήσω ἄλλους τόσους
ἀκούγοντας τὶς ρίζες νὰ προχωροῦν
μέσα στὸ ξερὸ χῶμα τῆς καρδιᾶς μου.

iv

In the dry soil of my heart
a cactus has grown.

It's been more than twenty centuries
since I dreamed of jasmine
my hair smelled of jasmine
my voice had taken something
of its delicate perfume
my clothes smelled of jasmine
my life had taken something
of its delicate perfume.

But the cactus is not bad;
it simply doesn't know it and is afraid.

Sadly I look at the cactus;
where did all those centuries go?

I will live as many again
listening to the roots
as they grow steadily
in the dry soil of my heart.

ν

Ἀνάμεσα σ' ἐμένα καὶ στὸν Ἥλιο
δὲν ὑπάρχει
πάρα μόνο ἡ διαφορά
τοῦ χρόνου

ἀνατέλλω καὶ δύω
ὑπάρχω καὶ δὲν ὑπάρχω

μὲ βλέπουν
χωρὶς νὰ δῶ τὸν ἑαυτό μου.

v

Between the sun and me
there is nothing
but the difference of time.

I rise and set
I exist and cease to be

they see me
though I cannot see myself.

vi

Ὅταν σταματήσει ὁ χρόνος
τὸ κελί μου γεμίζει μῆνες

μῆνες, μέρες, ὧρες, στιγμές

δέκατα δευτερολέπτων
δέκατα δευτερολέπτων
δέκατα δευτερολέπτων
ἕνα βῆμα πρὶν ἀπὸ τὸ χάος
ὑπάρχει χάος

ἕνα βῆμα μετὰ τὸ χάος
ὑπάρχει χάος

ἐγώ ὑπάρχω λίγο πρίν, λίγο μετά
ὑπάρχω μέσα στὸ χάος
δὲν ὑπάρχω

vi

When time stands still
my cell fills with months

months, days, hours, moments
tenths of a second
tenths of a second
tenths of a second
a step before chaos

there is chaos
a step before chaos

I exist a little before, a little after
I exist in chaos
I don't exist.

Protests against Theodorakis' arrest began in Europe, in the United States, where the score for *Zorba the Greek* had made him famous. Pete Seeger and Arthur Miller were among the artists calling for the composer's release.

The regime let Theodorakis out of prison and placed him under house arrest at his home in Vrachati. He immediately began writing articles and giving interviews to foreign journalists. The junta's solution was to move him to one of the most remote regions of Greece, the mountains of the Peloponnese. He spent the next eighteen months in Zatouna, in the province of Arcadia, writing music at an astonishing pace, but also seeking every possible way to smuggle messages to the outside world. His wife Myrto and the two children later joined him.

Theodorakis and his children in exile
Zatouna 1969

Yorgos was only nine years old, and both children hated going to the local elementary school where they stood out like pariahs. Having managed to smuggle a small tape-recorder into the village, Theodorakis recorded songs and messages on cassettes. Myrto then cut them into small strips, which she sewed into large cloth buttons on Yorgos's coat or into the hems of the children's clothing. When he went for a dentist's appointment in Athens, the strips of tape were removed from Yorgos's clothes, spliced together, and smuggled out of Greece.

It was one of these taped messages that found its way to the Greek exiles in Paris. Copies were sent to the groups of activists in Australia, Canada and the U.S. A group of Greeks sat in a comfortable house in suburban Melbourne and listened to the hoarse whisper of Theodorakis: *The village is small; barely twenty families live here. It is hemmed in on three sides by mountains...I have to go to the police station twice a day...*

every time I go out I'm escorted by two guards. I don't have the right to speak to anyone. Anyone who greets me is taking a risk; he's taken to the police station, searched and questioned.

When we first arrived, one of the guards forced my son, who is nine, to raise his arms and then he pushed him against a wall right in the center of the village and stripped him. When he got back to the house he was having convulsions ...these have recurred. We shall regain our liberty united with all peoples who are lovers of liberty! And let us not forget that Liberty is not a gift but something one wins by fighting for it!"

In 1970, after a pair of British journalists managed to reach Zatouna posing as tourists, Theodorakis was transferred again to the prison of Oropos, on the coast of Attica opposite Evia. For Theodorakis it was a welcome relief from the cold and isolation of Zatouna. In the prison, he was reunited with old comrades. He could see the sea. He taught the songs he had composed in Zatouna to his fellow prisoners and they formed a chorus. He started writing new songs. The winter passed, with protests, discussions about the future, music. One day in spring came news that some people had been seen standing on the dock singing a Theodorakis song. The composer, lying on his bunk in the prison hut, heard the song "Rosewater" with words by Nikos Gatsos:

Σε πότισα ροδόσταμο

Στον άλλο κόσμο που θα πας
κοίτα μη γίνεις σύννεφο
κοίτα μη γίνεις σύννεφο
κι άστρο πικρό της χαραυγής
και σε γνωρίσει η μάνα σου
που καρτερεί στην πόρτα

Σε πότισα ροδόσταμο
με πότισες φαρμάκι
της παγωνιάς αητόπουλο
της ερημιάς γεράκι

Πάρε μια βέργα λυγαριά
μια ρίζα δεντρολίβανο
μια ρίζα δεντρολίβανο
και γίνε φεγγαροδροσιά
να πέσεις τα μεσάνυχτα
στη διψασμένη αυλή σου

Σε πότισα ροδόσταμο
με πότισες φαρμάκι
της παγωνιάς αητόπουλο
της ερημιάς γεράκι

Rosewater

In the other world where you're going
be careful not to turn into a cloud
be careful not to turn into a cloud
and the bitter star of dawn
so your mother , waiting
at the door, will recognize you.

I sprinkled you with rosewater,
you watered me with poison
eagle of the frost
hawk of the desert.

Take a willow wand,
a root of rosemary,
a root of rosemary
and become the moon's dew
to fall as midnight tolls
on the thirsty courtyard

I sprinkled you with rosewater
you watered me with poison,
eagle of the frost
hawk of the desert.

Theodorakis went out with the other prisoners and stood by the barbed wire fence of the perimeter. In the distance, on a nearby jetty, he could make out three figures, one of whom he recognized by his unusual walk. It was the bouzouki-player Manolis Hiotis, the man who played on his first popular recording, *Epitaphios*. Hiotis was a legendary musician in Greece, not only for playing Theodorakis. Many considered him the greatest bouzouki player alive. Even the guards were reluctant to intervene and stop the performance on the jetty.

In his diary Theodorakis had recorded his first meeting with Hiotis when he was recording *Epitaphios*. "He took his bouzouki out of its case with great care. He held it tenderly, like a child. And then! Then the studio was filled with crystal springs and many-colored suns!"

The figures on the wharf finished their concert and moved slowly away, leaving Theodorakis so depressed that he could only stare at the ground. Next morning the newspapers carried the news that Manolis Hiotis had died of a heart attack.

Theodorakis's own health began to deteriorate. An attack of appendicitis caused him to be transferred to a prison hospital in Athens. Three days later he was called into the prison office. There a Greek army colonel was waiting, but there, strangely, was also Myrto, and behind her, a man who looked familiar — the French politician Jean-Jacques Servan-Schreiber. Nothing was explained, although Myrto's eyes told Theodorakis most of what he need to know, including the fact that this meeting would be their last for some time. Mystified, Theodorakis was driven to the airport where Servan-Schreiber's private jet was waiting. Myrto was not permitted to leave. It was the first day of his freedom, and the beginning of his life as an international symbol of resistance.

Mikis Theodorakis sitting on a bed in the
military hospital after being tortured.

(From the song-cycle *Arcadia X*)

Είχα τρεις ζωές

Είχα τρεις ζωές. Τη μια την πήρε ο άνεμος,
την άλλη οι βροχές κι η τρίτη μου ζωή
κλεισμένη σε δυο βλέμματα πνίγηκε μες στο δάκρυ.

Έμεινα μόνος χωρίς ζωή, χωρίς ζωές,
τη μια την πήρε ο άνεμος την άλλη οι βροχές.
Έμεινα μόνος, εγώ κι ο Δράκος στη μεγάλη σπηλιά.

Κρατώ ρομφαία, κρατώ σπαθί.
Εγώ θα σε πνίξω, εγώ θα σε σκοτώσω,
εγώ θα σε σβήσω, εγώ θα σε τινάξω πάνω απ' τη ζωή μου.

Γιατί έχω τρεις ζωές.
Η μια για να πονάει,
η άλλη για να θέλει,
κι η τρίτη για να νικά.

I Had Three Lives

Song and lyric by Theodorakis, composed in exile in Zatouna

I had three lives; the wind took one
the rain the other and my third life
shut in behind two eyelids, was drowned in tears.

I was left alone without a life, without lives,
the wind took one, the rain the other;
I was left alone, I and the Dragon in the great cave.

I hold a scimitar, I hold a sword
I'll drown you, I'll kill you
I'll obliterate you, I'll blow you up.

Because I have three lives,
one to suffer with
one to wish with
and the third to win with.

4. Exile.

There were dark smudges under the man's eyes, and I found myself staring at him often as the discussions went on. I was shocked by what has happened to him, but to be honest, I also found him attractive as only a deeply troubled man can be. I never said a word to him, but as he left the room he took one hand out of his pocket, reached for my hand as if to shake it, and in a gesture so swift I doubt if anyone in the room noticed, he put something in it. I knew not to open my hand until he had disappeared. When I was sure no eyes were on me, I relaxed my fingers. On my palm lay a *komboloi*, a set of dark blue ceramic beads strung on worn leather.

In retrospect, the gesture was typical of the dictatorship. Greeks who were involved with the resistance spent their days in danger, often in pain, but the drama of their lives gave every encounter an added intensity. A pair of eyes that sought your face too often could be erotic as well as dangerous. The brief meeting helped make my life as a relief teacher at Putney Comprehensive School in London bearable. I walked into the classroom, one hand in my pocket, fingering the beads of my *komboloi* and nothing the students did could damage me. I began taking kids out into the corridor, one by one, while the others made havoc in the classroom and asking them about their lives. One told me he was a trained auto-body man and could be earning his living in a garage if he weren't forced to go to school. Another said she came to school because if she didn't her father beat her. In the classroom, the students became part of an aggressive mob. Individually, they were often a pleasure to talk to. I turned the worn beads over in my hand and dreamed of Greece.

One night there was a concert in Chalk Farm, an area where many of London's large Greek Cypriot population lived. Maria Farandouri, a young woman who had been singing with Theodorakis on the night of the *coup d'état* and a male singer, Andonis Kaloyannis, were performing his music at a large auditorium called The Round House. Greeks filled the hall to its wooden rafters and as the lights went down a slim Greek girl dressed in black limped onto the platform followed by a handsome bearded man. When she began to sing her deep voice sounded as if it belonged to a woman twice her age. The audience was silent, absorbing not only the beauty of the music, but the poignancy of the fact that the man who had written it was in jail, his music forbidden in their country. Men and women around me were weeping, and I was soon weeping with them. By the end of the evening we felt we could have toppled the dictatorship with the sheer force of our emotion:

Είναι μεγάλος ο γιαλός, είναι μακρύ το κύμα
Είναι μεγάλος ο καϋμός, είναι πικρό το κρίμα...

The shore is large, the wave is long;
the sorrow is great, the crime is bitter...

Maria sang, and we sang with her, our voices hoarse, our hearts pounding. Walking out into the drizzling rain of the London street we were in a state of exhilaration. The dictatorship was terrible, but it had created this, this fierce chorus, this love of Greece that united us as a single body.

Some days after my night at the Roundhouse I was walking along Tottenham Court Road and noticed a headline on one of the tabloids displayed beside the tube station: "Women Prisoners Tell of Torture in Greek Prisons." Reluctantly, I bought the paper and began to read.

The reports that had been smuggled out of Greece to British journalists made me feel so nauseous I had to lean against a lamp post for support. I folded the newspaper and stuffed it in my bag like a piece of pornography. I understood why the tabloid press had suddenly focused its attention on Greece. To describe torture, especially the torture of women, is always a form of pornography. Years later I would go to hear Beverly Allen, author of a book about the Bosnian War called *Rape Warfare*, talk about the use of rape as a weapon of war. "I refuse to speak about the details of torture used by the Chetniks," she said. "I don't want to risk being titillating."

I felt suddenly ashamed to have been enjoying the music of Theodorakis, and the meetings with fine-eyed young Greeks in the anti-dictatorship movement. I wanted to do something more meaningful, but what? Smuggle guns to the resistance? Take secret messages? And what if they arrested me? I wasn't brave enough to face even the thought of torture.

Two British women helped answer my dilemma. Someone had told me the women were working to help the families of political prisoners in Greece. Together they had formed something called the Greek Relief Fund, whose purpose was to send money to the families of prisoners. They were the only people in England who had complete files of all Greek political prisoners. A day later I called their office in Soho and asked could I come and talk to them. I knew nothing about them, or that one was Marion Sarafis, widow of the legendary leader of ELAS, the partisan army that had led the resistance to the Germans in the mountains of Greece. The woman who answered my knock at the door of the tiny office at 26 Goodge Street was her partner in the organization, Diana Pym. She greeted me with kindly impatience.

"Look," she said when I'd made my speech about wanting to do something to help the Greek cause. "Don't try to be a heroine. You'll only get people into trouble. We made the mistake of giving a Swedish girl a contact, and she was followed by the police wherever she went. You look more like a Greek than she did but you're not. If you're serious about doing something for Greece, go back to your own country and see what you can do there. You can help publicize what's happening there, write letters to the paper, things like that. If you go via Greece you can take some money or a single message for us perhaps, but after that you'd be a liability to anyone you met."

I felt foolish and naïve. At the time, I hadn't thought of going back to Australia, but the sensible Ms. Pym had sown a seed. Sitting around singing Theodorakis songs no longer seemed quite so exciting, and the quarrels that had broken out between the various groups of exiles in London made their talk of resistance less persuasive.

It was winter when T. and I set out, and too cold to travel by motorcycle. Instead, we bought an old blue Bedford van that had been used to transport less serious patients to the hospital; it would serve us as a camper and still leave enough room for the motorcycle in the back. George Papandreou, the Prime Minister whose resignation set in motion the events that culminated in the coup d'état, had died in November, 1968. Two months earlier there had been a referendum on a new constitution legitimizing the military regime. Since the country was under martial law and the media were tightly censored, it was not surprising that the result was an overwhelming endorsement of the dictatorship, especially since the ballot-boxes were carefully watched and the ballots printed, in some villages, on different colored paper, blue for yes, pink for no.

The funeral of George Papandreou took place in the Metropolitan Cathedral in Athens in the aftermath of the compromised ballot, and hundreds of thousands of people crowded into the downtown streets, some calling out "Here is your 'No,'" others chanting "Get up, old man, and see us!" Some were arrested, but the crowds were so large that it was difficult for the police to intervene. Naturally, the Greek Press had nothing exceptional to report the next day. But a photographer, hidden in a building near the Cathedral, had taken pictures of the crowd and the London exiles had produced a small booklet with reports of the funeral and clear photographs of the sea of placard-carrying mourners around the Cathedral.

When we left London, I carried dozens of the booklets in my luggage. My mother's best friend met us en route and traveled with us through Yugoslavia. She was six feet tall, white-haired and impeccably dressed, so I gave her the seditious literature to carry over the border in her handbag. As an old radical , she was delighted to be useful to the cause. A few days later in Athens I delivered them to the address I had been given and heard no more. Nikos, who had given me the booklets, had also asked me to contact two men in Crete, leftists who were now constantly watched by representatives of the junta. "If you can," he said, "go to the village and tell them we're doing what we can outside Greece. Tell them we haven't forgotten them."

It was a small gesture and an excuse to visit Crete, even in the dictatorship, so T. and I set out on the motorcycle the next week and took the night ferry to Crete. The village Nikos sent us to on the side of Mt. Psiloritis was known for its lyra-players. I had looked forward to hearing some Cretan music as well as playing a bit part in the drama of the dictatorship, but a few days before we reached the village two teenagers had been killed by lightning as they sat out on the mountainside watching their sheep. The whole village was silent, mourning the boys' deaths.

It was hard to explain what we were doing in the village when we arrived. I was careful not to make direct inquiries about the two men I wanted to meet, so we pretended to be a couple of more-than-usually well-informed travelers who had heard about the music of the village from a friend in London. We sat in a café, feeling conspicuous and a little foolish. I had already made myself notorious by trying to stop two boys from stoning a dog to death on the village garbage heap. The dog had chased some chickens and eaten one and had been handed over to the boys for execution. I could hear yelping and went over to see what was happening. The dog was already bleeding and too weak to run for its life. I yelled at the boys who took no notice of me until a thin man with a sad moustache intervened, driving them away temporarily in order not to offend the visitor. I knew the dog would die that night but I couldn't watch it another moment.

I asked the man who'd intervened if he knew M. "Who wants him?" he asked, his face expressionless. "He's a friend of a friend in London," I said.

In the taverna that night, as he brought us a plate of snails, the waiter surprised me with a quiet remark:

"Eleven o'clock, tomorrow. M. will meet you at the *cafeneon* near the bus station in Platanos." Then he disappeared.

Again I had the feeling I was in a movie. Did people really say such things? The atmosphere in the restaurant was gloomy, and nobody appeared to take any notice of us. We left and went to a dank hotel to sleep. The next morning we rode the motorcycle down the mountain to the café and found the thin man who had temporarily intervened in the dog-killing sitting at a table with another man. It was one of those unattractive, noisy Greek cafes, full of smoke, music, shouting, and the clatter of plastic backgammon pieces. I realized that I had brought the two villagers on an expensive bus-trip from their village and that my message was meaningless. "Nikos sends greetings. The Greeks are organized in London and Paris. They're doing whatever they can to make the world aware of what's happening here. Nikos wants to know how things are in the village."

The men showed no sign of pleasure at my news, but the thin man who chose to speak told me that the situation was very serious.

"In the early days, after the coup, the local policemen couldn't do much. They were our friends — we've known them since they were children. Now they've sent all the Cretan *horofylakes* to Macedonia, and they've sent Macedonians to Crete. They know we don't like the Macedonians and they don't like us, so they planted them here and our boys there. That way they can make the police inform on us. We have to watch what we say up in the village. That's why we met you here. Tell Nikos about this, tell him things are bad here."

The man had been talking in a low voice, but curious eyes were turned in our direction and we began making small talk until the bus arrived. The two men were taking the bus back to the village, but they paid for our coffee as they left. I knew better than to argue.

I wondered, later, about the meeting. Did it mean something to the two men? Did it put them at risk? Was I, as Diana Pym suggested, a liability? It was worth something, perhaps, to know that the outside world was concerned, but it was small comfort in the life of the village. The two men, according to Nikos, were the most active in the resistance. Resistance is not just a dangerous activity; it may cause more harm than good. Men like these would have been responsible, together with their British leaders, for the assassination of German officers here during the war. Such acts, it can be argued, tied units of the German army down as they hunted for the perpetrators. Possibly it contributed infinitesimally to the defeat of Rommel in North Africa. But the reprisals were terrible. Whole villages were razed to the ground, the male population executed, the women and children left homeless and destitute. If your husband or son were responsible for such an act, would you be proud?

*   *   *

I had moved to Sydney, become a journalist for a national paper and a student of harpsichord at the New South Wales Conservatorium. Both skills would serve me well in my later Greek life. Working as a music critic for a national newspaper gave me the opportunity to also write about the dictatorship and about Theodorakis. Learning the harpsichord became my entrée into performing in Greek bands.

I soon discovered that the Sydney Greek activists were divided between what the Melbourne Greeks called the *stenokefali* (the narrow-minded Stalinist communists) and the moderate opposition. There were constant battles between them on tactics and who to invite to Australia to speak, but no-one had any doubts about the visit of Theodorakis. By the time the "Committee for the Restoration of Democracy in Greece" left for the airport on a winter's day in 1972, animosities between the quarreling Greek factions were suspended and we were all in a state of euphoria. The terminal at Sydney Airport was packed with Greeks, Australian Labor Party politicians, and reporters shouting at one another. Suddenly, over all their heads rose the head of the man Greeks generally referred to as "The Tall One."

To be a head and shoulders taller than one's fellow countrymen is not always an advantage – when bullets are flying around at a demonstration, for example. For Theodorakis, who reached almost his full height of 6 foot 4 inches in early adolescence, it was a terrible embarrassment to be so tall. But when you are already a hero, or a politician, stature is an added attraction. I watched the head move through the crowd of Greeks who were shouting "Mikis!" "Mikis!" and recognized the face I had first seen in a restaurant in the Plaka. An Australian politician who knew me slightly as a journalist pulled me into the VIP lounge where police were endeavoring to steer Theodorakis for a press conference. It may have been a measure of the Greeks' state of disorganization or simply the excitement of the occasion that no-one had thought to arrange for an interpreter. The politician pushed me into the vacant chair beside Theodorakis and said with a leery smile, "You interpret — the Press want to see a pretty girl, not a local Greek."

I was as ill-prepared to interpret for Theodorakis at a press conference as I would have been to referee a football game, and I remember very little about what was said except my overwhelming sense of inadequacy and Theodorakis's humorous asides that rescued me from complete paralysis and charmed everyone. The man sitting next to me may have been legend, but he was informally dressed in a navy blue wind breaker and in contrast to me, completely at ease with reporters and cameras. All

Theodorakis and the author at a press conference at Sydney airport in 1972.

the Greeks addressed him like an old friend as "Mikis". There were questions about the resistance in Europe, about his escape, about the length of time he expected the dictatorship to last. Somehow I stumbled through the conference, Theodorakis was delivered to his hotel, and I was able to comprehend the fact that legends could wear ordinary clothes and make jokes.

It was at the concert the next night that I saw the Theodorakis I expected, a figure who loomed like a giant raven before his musicians, his hands curved forward in two arcs that seemed to draw the music from them on hidden strings. The songs we heard were not the sort of music his audiences were used to. He called some of them 'flow-songs' and they were very different from Greek popular songs. They were settings of Greek poets and of his own poems, including a long sequence of poems written in Bouboulinas Prison, while he waited from day to day for torture or execution. One group of songs was dedicated to Andreas Lendakis, a fellow prisoner in Bouboulinas Jail who had been badly tortured. Tapping on the wall of their cells, the two men had worked out a code of communication. Andreas described his interrogation: sand-bags to the head, iron bars to the soles of the feet. Theodorakis told him of his plan to go on a hunger strike. Later, in the brief interlude of house arrest at Vrachati, Theodorakis would write four "Songs for Andreas." It was one of the few times Theodorakis sang himself that night, as if unwilling to entrust these songs to another voice:

Το Σφαγείο

Το μεσημέρι χτυπάνε στο γραφείο
μετρώ τους χτύπους τον πόνο μετρώ
είμαι θρεφτάρι μ' έχουν κλείσει στο σφαγείο
σήμερα εσύ αύριο εγώ

Χτυπούν το βράδυ στην ταράτσα τον Ανδρέα
μετρώ τους χτύπους το αίμα μετρώ
πίσω απ' τον τοίχο πάλι θα `μαστε παρέα
τακ τακ εσύ τακ τακ εγώ

Που πάει να πει
σ' αυτή τη γλώσσα τη βουβή
βαστάω γερά, κρατάω καλά

Μες στις καρδιές μας αρχιναέι το πανηγύρι
τακ τακ εσύ τακ τακ εγώ
τακ τακ εσύ τακ τακ εγώ

Μύρισε το σφαγείο μας θυμάρι
και το κελί μας κόκκινο ουρανό
Μύρισε το σφαγείο μας θυμάρι
και το κελί μας κόκκινο ουρανό

To hear the song visit goo.gl/rfbqvT

The Slaughterhouse

At noon they beat in the office,
I count the blows, I measure the blood.
I am a beast locked in the slaughterhouse,
you, today, me tomorrow.

In the evening they beat Andreas on the terrace,
I count the blows, I measure the pain.
We'll meet again behind the wall,
tap-tap, you, tap-tap, me .

In our dumb language this means
I'm bearing up, I'm holding on.

In our hearts the celebration begins
tap-tap you, tap-tap me
tap-tap you, tap-tap me

In our hearts the festival begins,
tap-tap, you, tap-tap, me.
Our slaughterhouse smelled of thyme,
our cell, red sky.

At such moments you understand the chasm that separates those who grew up in relative comfort and peace from those who have been tortured and imprisoned. The corner of the curtain is raised and you peer into the darkest regions of the human soul. It is only bearable because of the music, the language of poetry, but it is unimaginable without it. The "Songs for Andreas" were among the angriest of the evening, but there were also melancholy songs composed in Zatouna, and lyrical settings of Seferis's *Mythistorema* composed in Averof Prison. When we emerged into the mild Sydney night we were all silenced for a time. My life, I thought, will never be the same. I was not alone. Nobody who attended a Theodorakis concert during the dictatorship would forget the intensity of the experience. An Israeli woman I met still carried her ticket to one of his concerts in her pocket ten years afterwards.

Before he left Sydney I invited Theodorakis and his musicians to my house for dinner. He immediately noticed the harpsichord and asked me if I played, but it was his pianist Yiannis Didilis who persuaded me to play. He had consumed a great deal of wine by then, and sat down on the stool beside me as I nervously fumbled my way through the slow movement of Bach's *Italian Concerto*. Didilis was so excited he took off his shirt and we all began to dance. Soon Theodorakis's shirt was off too and the two of them beamed and sweated in their undershirts. As he left, Theodorakis said "When the dictatorship falls, you'll play harpsichord in my orchestra." It was the sort of thing you say at a party when the wine is flowing. That it was a genuine offer never occurred to me.

5. Return

The Modern Greek word for torture: *vasano*, has only changed from the ancient in pronunciation. The original meaning of the word was a touchstone, a dark stone on which gold, when rubbed, left a unique mark. From the literal meaning of testing gold came the metaphorical use of the word as a form of testing the truth of an assertion. In fifth century BC Athens, the cradle — as we're so often reminded — of democracy, male and female slaves were regularly tortured to obtain evidence against their masters in lawsuits. The evidence extracted by torture was regarded as indisputably true. As valuable pieces of property that might be damaged by the various machines used in the process, slaves could not be tortured without the permission of their owners. But to refuse to have your slave tortured was tantamount to an admission of guilt.

*   *   *

There was only one attempt to assassinate one of the leaders of the junta, and that was made by a young mathematics student, Alekos Panagoulis. He planted a bomb under a bridge on the road from Athens to the airport. Colonel Papadopoulos's car drove over it just a few moments too late. Panagoulis was caught because a planned escape boat left without waiting for him. His inhuman torture lasted for months on end. The Italian journalist Oriana Falacci, who fell in love with him, spares no detail of it in the book she wrote about him, *A Man*. Intervention from world leaders, including the Pope, saved Panagoulis from the death sentence, and he was reprieved before the dictatorship ended, but he died in a car crash soon after the restoration of democracy, a victim, according to Falacci and others who knew him, of a neo-fascist organization with members in Italy and Greece.

If the bomb had gone off a few seconds later, the dictatorship might have ended, or it might have become worse. A non-violent demonstration by students of the Athens Polytechnic in November 1973, on the anniversary of the death of George Papandreou, was more effective; its brutal suppression probably contributed to the fall of the regime. Panagoulis and the students of the Polytechnic became heroes. Heroes don't have to be effective. Inspiration is enough to make myths from.

Eleni Vlachou, owner and editor of one of Greece's famous newspapers, escaped over the Greek border wearing a wig and dark glasses. The first editorial she wrote on her return was not about the joy of coming home or anything else her readers expected but about her cat, Poopsy, who had been an independent-minded animal before the coup. Now, Poopsy seemed to lack her former spirit. She had become a mild, obedient house-cat, the result, her owner suspected, of seven years of cultural stultification.

It was true that there was an odd mood in the city, a feeling of nostalgia, nostalgia for the moral certainty of the dictatorship when the good were good and the bad were bad. Black and white politics had turned grey, as if they had been put through the wash together. No-one seemed to feel that justice would be done in the upcoming trial of the leaders of the dictatorship. How could any punishment restore the seven years Greece had lost? Who was responsible for such a step backwards into mindless, provincial, puritanical stagnation? Was it the CIA? The Left? Or was it just a group of mid-level army officers with grandiose ambitions? And if it was, how did they get away with it? Were the Greeks asleep?

Amnesty is a Greek word that has to do with the political necessity for forgetting. For the ancient Greeks, amnesty was the political expedient for something the leaders of Athens knew they could not cure, *alaston penthos* : incurable grief. Herodotus tells us that when

Phrynikhou produced a play called *The Capture of Miletos*, a tragedy in which he described the destruction of that Ionian town by the Persians, the Athenian audience all burst into tears. Phrynichus was fined five thousand drachmae for "reminding them of their own misfortunes," and any future performance of the play was banned. From then on, tragedians learned that when they wanted to write about misfortunes, they had better remove their sad tales from the contemporary scene and situate them in a mythical past. A similar ban, imposed in the year 403 BCE was passed by the democrats who had returned to Athens after the city's defeat at the hands of the Spartans. The government declared an amnesty, forbidding people to "recall the misfortunes" of the dictatorship that preceded their return. The wounds of the dictatorship could not be cured, they reasoned, but if they were not talked about, there was a hope that they would not lead to civil unrest.

How would the modern Greek state deal with its immediate and shameful past now that a civilian regime, under the old conservative leader Constantine Karamanlis, had taken charge? Would they declare an amnesty and try to erase the memory of mass arrests, killings, torture, exile, and censorship? Would there be retribution? Or would a civilized modern trial take place? And who would be tried? The whole military junta? Its leaders? The head of the Military Police, who ordered the worst tortures, or the younger officers who carried out his orders?

It would take a year before the machinery of justice was prepared to deal with the incurable grief caused by the dictatorship. By then a new Greece was getting on with life as usual. Women were buying the latest shoes on Stadiou Street, tourists swarmed the islands like a plague of Australian red ants, workers came back from Germany driving Mercedes taxis, bouzouki clubs were jammed till the small hours, private cars, thousands of them, squeezed into a city with no garages, and were parked on sidewalks by their impatient drivers. For some Greeks it was a time of euphoria, for others, a time of anger. Some wanted to forget the junta years, others to see justice done, especially for the brutal events of November 1973. A Dutch television crew had managed to film the occupation of the Athens Polytechnic, and had captured the moment when a tank broke down the gates of the university, opening the way for police and army units to enter the compound and open fire on the students. Each night the film was screened four or five times in the small apartment of a member of parliament who lived nearby. I sat with some of the students who had been inside the university on that November day and we gasped in unison as the tank smashed its way through the high metal gates and the police started firing into the crowd of students.

Korydalos Prison, August 1975.

A heavily made-up blond in a white pantsuit pushes past to get to her seat in the improvised Press box. Her eyes are a fierce green. She fixes Colonel Papadopoulos, leader of the 1967 coup, with a glare that might have disemboweled a more sensitive man. As her lips curl down in disgust I recognize her: it is Melina Mercouri, who has managed to obtain a journalist's pass from a Canadian newspaper to attend the court where members of the junta are on trial.

The trial of the Colonels. In the press box, L to R : Alekos Panagoulis (the man who tried to assassinate Colonel Papadopoulos), Melina Mercouri, a Dutch journalist, the author

"Hey, Mr Papadopoulos, won't you talk to me?" she yells. On the far side of Melina sits Alekos Panagoulis, the man who tried to assassinate Papadopoulos and was brutally tortured before his release. I am glad that Melina cuts off my view of him. A photograph of him taken just after his arrest showed a young, handsome student with frightened eyes. Now he looks like a middle-aged man. His torturers were recently interviewed in the newspapers and said they didn't understand how he could still be alive after what they'd done to him for months on end.

For a week I have watched the trial of the dictators on closed circuit television in the basement of the Grand Bretagne Hotel, but a Dutch journalist friend has suggested we go together to the court today because most of the foreign correspondents have already left; it will be less crowded and we should find a seat. Nothing has prepared me for the strange atmosphere of this courtroom. It is one of the most unusual trials ever held in Europe, or anywhere else for that matter. The twenty defendants are accused of high treason, not by the State but by a group of independent Greek lawyers.

Five judges sit on a raised dais with the prosecutor while the defense lawyers speak from the body of the court. Most of them quickly deny the legality of the court and withdraw, saying their clients will not offer any defense. The President of the court asks one of the few who remain to undertake the defense of all the remaining defendants.

The first witness draws a shocked murmur from the court. He is a handsome, middle-aged man with a neat goatee. The attendants wheel him into the room and bend the microphones down over his chair. At the time of the coup he was teaching in the Military Academy in Athens and was said to be the most decorated man in the Army. He was imprisoned by the junta for his loyalty to the king. His injuries are not the result of torture but an attempt to escape by jumping from a prison window; nevertheless they have a strong effect on the court.

Most of the men who carried out the torture, members of the notorious Military Police, are being tried in a separate court. We have watched this trial, too, on closed-circuit television. The witnesses begin their testimony in a controlled tone but end in tears or collapse. Lady Amalia Fleming, the Greek widow of the discoverer of penicillin, describes her ordeal in a calm voice, but begins to falter under cross-examination. A woman dentist gives testimony on behalf of her husband who has lost the power of speech but stands beside her making animal-like noises. She describes her first sight of her husband, forty-eight days after his arrest. She saw an unrecognizable creature lying on the floor covered with wounds and bruises who barely understood her.

The accused sit on rows of chairs. They are dressed in neatly-pressed uniforms and look like any young Greek men you see directing traffic on a street corner or guarding the Acropolis. They listen to the testimony without registering any emotion. Each one of them has caused excruciating pain to another human being, each one has reduced a fellow-Greek to something less than human.

Trial of the colonels. Between the guards, Papadopoulos, Makarezos, Pattakos, Spandidakis. Witness: Mavros.

Despite its bizarre nature, the trial is, I realize, both necessary and salutary. Since the state neglected to bring the colonels and their allies to justice, the lawyers have stepped in to make sure that the public in Greece and beyond is aware that an illegal regime has been ruling Greece for seven years. Each testimony describes a personal agony but together they add up to a consistent story. The myth that Greece was threatened by a possible Communist take-over has been dispelled by witnesses from the political Right as well as the Left. The colonels' claim to be stepping in to avoid such a crisis has been discredited. The judges will ask for the maximum sentences for the defendants knowing the sentences will be commuted. The very fact that the leaders have been in jail for a year awaiting trial is already something that surprises the Greeks who presumed that they had cut a deal with Karamanlis not to be brought to trial.

The Greek state may have wished to resort to the ancient cure of amnesty, but a group of lawyers pre-empted the desire for forgetting. The trial was, in sense, a show without serious consequences for the accused, but it allowed the *alaston penthos* of seven years to be displayed in public, tears to be shed, a necessary *catharsis* to be achieved.

In the spring, Theodorakis with Maria Farandouri and his band, toured the Greek countryside. The tour began in the north, where the weather was still cold. It was the first time the composer had visited the country towns of Greece since his return. He had given one concert in a stadium at the end of the summer, and had spent much of his winter recording the music he had written over the seven years of the dictatorship. I had been reluctant to contact him in Athens, knowing that he was surrounded by admirers, journalists and old friends, but I realized that if I caught a bus from Athens in the early morning, I could attend his concert in the town of Kozani. It was a ten hour bus-ride, but in a small town it would be easier to talk to him, and I could write an article for the paper I worked for in Australia, about the way he and his music were being received after a seven year absence.

The journey was long, the town was dark, and the hotel cheerless. I wondered why I had traveled all this way instead of trying to see Theodorakis in Athens but I was curious to see the reaction of the audience to one of his concerts. I hurried to the theater only to find there were no tickets left. An angry crowd had gathered outside demanding to be let in. Having traveled so far I was not going to miss the concert. I forgot my diffidence and called the hotel where Theodorakis was staying. I was told not to worry, just to give my name to the people at the box office. The concert was supposed to begin in fifteen minutes. There was no time to eat. I ran to the theater and squeezed to the front of the crowd where an envelope with my name on it was already waiting. Of course the concert didn't start on time, but it was worth sitting in the theater to see the excited faces of the crowd and share their anticipation as they waited for Mikis to appear.

The concert had all the drama of the concerts I had been to in Australia, but the audience's reaction grew more intense as the evening progressed. By the end of the performance they rose as one and headed towards the stage. Technicians were calling out a phrase I would become familiar with over the next months "Cables! Watch the cables!" I was afraid there would be a riot or someone would be electrocuted. Everyone wanted to reach out a hand and touch this mythical man whose music had been their secret weapon against the regime. A song hummed *sotto voce* had told a neighbor where you stood, a few notes on a bouzouki suggested a forbidden tune, and all eyes looked nervously to see if a sinister figure in dark glasses was standing nearby. And here was the man who had created the songs they'd hummed under their breath, or sung together in jail. Theodorakis towered above the audience, his hair wild, a huge smile on his face, grasping a hand there, embracing an old friend and fellow-prisoner there until he could get to his dressing-room. I waited until the first crush had left and worked my way to the back of the room. I hated feeling like a groupie, but if I were to be one, this was a man worth lining up for. He raised his eyes and saw me.

"Gail," he said, with a smile. "You, here in Kozani? How did you get here? Do you have a harpsichord?"

I looked at him with some amusement.

"A harpsichord? Not here."

"In Athens?"

"Not yet."

"Find one and you're in the band," he said. "We'll be going on a tour of the Peloponnese next month."

My head and heart were racing in tandem. Was he serious? If so, how could I get a harpsichord? There weren't any to be had in Athens, or not the sort you could travel with. And did I dare play with Theodorakis? I would surely be exposed as a mediocre musician in front of the man I admired more than anyone in the world. How would I learn all the new music I didn't know? But if I said no, would I, like D.H. Lawrence, lose "my chance with one of the lords /of life?"

"I'll see what I can do," I said.

My mother, who was not always sympathetic to the choices I made, rescued me. She was visiting friends in London. I called her and asked her to try to find the smallest possible harpsichord in London and ship it to me immediately. In retrospect, it was astonishing that she found one. It was a spinet, she told me, but the only affordable or portable instrument she could find. I rarely asked my mother for anything, but when I did, I knew she would deliver. If I had asked her to meet me in Nairobi Airport at 4 a.m. on a Saturday morning with a gun in her handbag, she would have turned up half an hour early, lit a cigarette, ordered a whisky from the bar if there was one, and sat down to wait for me, a revolver tucked between her powder compact and her handkerchief.

There were no rehearsals and I'd had no time to even unpack the spinet before it was loaded onto a truck. I was to meet the other members of the band at a small square near Leoforos Alexandras at nine and we would all take a private bus to Pylos. By 9.15 there was no sign of the bus, but the two bouzouki players and a guitarist were there and we sat on the pavement drinking coffee. By 9.30 half the band had arrived and Maria Farandouri stepped out of a taxi wearing a long denim skirt and tie-dyed shirt. No-one had paid any attention to us until now, but she was one of the best-known singers in Greece and every record store had half a dozen photographs of her in its window, so people stopped to stare at us. An old gypsy musician went to the street corner and began to play his clarinet. He was a good player, but the younger musicians were more interested in the girls hurrying by on their way to work. Each girl was discussed noisily.

"Go carefully with those eggs!"

"Great balconies you've got!"

"Move that body, Doll!"

"Give us a kiss, Sweetheart!"

By 10.30 everyone was restless. The bus hadn't arrived and no-one remembered the tour manager's phone number. They started calling other people who might know, and at 10.45 the bus finally appeared. We climbed aboard, the musicians with their instruments and everyone with suitcases. Theodorakis hadn't appeared and someone remembered we were supposed to collect him an hour ago at his parents' house.

When we got to Nea Smyrni, we couldn't find the house. We drove up and down narrow suburban streets, and finally came to the right house, but there was no-one at home. Then the same person who remembered we were supposed to collect him recalled that we were to meet him on the corner of the street. By now we were running two hours late and I couldn't imagine that Theodorakis would still be there. But when we turned the corner, he was standing with his father on the sidewalk as if the two of them had nothing else to do. He climbed aboard greeting everyone by name and beaming at us. It had been a long time since breakfast so everyone took advantage of the stop to buy ice-creams. Theodorakis's two children climbed on the bus with us, and he sat up near the front going over his press cuttings. He also handed me a pile of scores for his songs that I thought would solve some of my problems, not having had a single rehearsal, nor seen a note of music.

It was early May. The ugly outskirts of Athens disappeared behind us in a pall of yellow smoke and dust and the waters of the Saronic Gulf sparkled ahead. Poppies bloodied the fields and roses drooped, heavy with scent, over village houses. As we neared Corinth Theodorakis announced, "It's nearly time for lunch. We'll have lunch at my place. It's still shut up, but the local taverna will send us food."

By now the sun was quite hot, and the bus bumped along a dirt road before coming to a stop some distance from the house. We all climbed out and walked the rest of the way to the garden of a large stone villa beside the sea. The size of it surprised me. Mikis pointed proudly to the three-storey tower at the corner of the house where his studio was, and to the duck pond, still under construction. He greeted the workmen and we sat down at a stone table under the tree. He pointed out the wine barrels nearby labeled with the names of some of his heroes: "This one's Karl Marx," he said. "Let's try some."

Bread and cheese appeared and we broke off large chunks as the pinkish mountain wine flowed. When we'd had enough we moved on, but not to the highway. Instead we headed down the road to the local taverna for some more food. Some of the musicians tried to pay for the food, but today everything was on "uncle" Mikis, who, by this, time, was composing a little song in English for my benefit, and introducing all the naughty words he knew into the lyrics.

It was already 6.30 when we arrived. The concert was scheduled to begin at nine. While most of the musicians headed for the hotel to sleep off their lunch, I raced for the football stadium where the concert would take place. The spinet was still in its packing case, and when we opened it we saw that it had been seriously damaged. It looked as if someone had delivered a mortal blow to the soundboard, which had a gaping hole in it. One of the strings was broken and some of the keys were jammed. I was in despair, but one of the technicians suggested that a bouzouki string might work, or two joined together. Fortunately bouzouki strings can be bought at the kiosks that occupy most street corners in Greek towns and stock a surprising number of useful things. It took two hours to coax the spinet to work. The bouzouki string was pure genius, but the instrument would not hold its tune. By now it was getting cold but there was no time to go back to the hotel and change. By 9 o'clock the stadium was filled with four thousand people and hundreds crowded around the entrance complaining that they couldn't get in. When Mikis arrived, he told the organizers to let the people in free to sit on the grass. The crowd poured forward, dangerously close to cables and lights.

I was shivering as I tried to work out the order of the program. When I ran my fingers over some of the pieces the pianist told me I wasn't in the right key. Farandouri's voice had deepened and they were playing everything a tone lower. I frantically tried to work out the chords, paralyzed by terror and cold. The instrument was rapidly going out of tune but the noise was so deafening there was no way I could tune. At interval, a film crew lit the stage with a battery of glaring spotlights while I struggled to adjust the spinet. I tried to join in all the songs I knew. Sometimes I would hit a wrong note or not realize that the order had been changed. I felt I had been exposed as a musical fool and I longed for the ordeal to end.

As we packed up our instruments, the crowd surged onto the stage nearly knocking us off our seats in an attempt to reach Theodorakis. Musicians who had had their instruments smashed in previous concerts warned me to hold on tight to the spinet. I hugged it to me and ducked my head as frantic fans poured over and around me and technicians shouted "The cables! Watch the cables!"

As the tour went on this became the common finale to the concerts. Mikis was a legend to these audiences, and everyone wanted to touch him. Nothing would stop the human lava that flowed towards him, and only when he left the stage could we safely pack up our instruments and get on the bus.

I might have known that we would always be running late, that the rehearsals we had been promised before the next concert, mostly for my benefit, would be cut so short that all I had time to do was find out the program and arrange the scores in some order. On the bus I had penciled in new keys, but no one really wanted to be bothered with such details;

they were busy gossiping or dozing. They were used to the celebrity life, especially the singers, Maria, Petros Pandis, a tall leonine baritone, and a dark bearded singer, Andonis Kaloyiannis. Singers are invariably the stars of such groups, and Farandouri was a legendary performer.

I hadn't realized, until I played in Theodorakis's band, just how sexy stardom was. I had associated panting groupies with rock bands. I hadn't really thought about the sexiness of political heroes. Between the music and the politics, Theodorakis and his singers had become something like a cross between Che Guevara and the Beatles. Over the next weeks, as we played in large and small towns in the Peloponnese, filling football stadiums and theaters to overflowing, sex oozed around us. It was directed mostly towards Theodorakis and his singers, but it spilled over, catching bouzouki-players and guitar-players in its flow. We were hot by association, and girls lined up outside the dressing-rooms, waiting for anyone who would sign an autograph or offer something more. One night a young man asked me to sign the plaster cast on his broken arm.

"Why me?" I asked. "Because you're in the band," he answered.

I'd become a peripheral star on the edge of the galaxy, bright by association.

A pattern emerged to our days. The sold-out stadiums, the crush of people at the end of the performance threatening our instruments and the electric cables,

Volos, 1975. Pianist Kostas Ganoselis gives me a quick lesson before the performance in a football stadium.

arguments that seem to get more heated as the tour went on between Theodorakis and young Communists who thought he was disloyal to the Party, the lines of girls, one or two of whom would generally turn up at the restaurants where we ate after the concerts, old friends of Theodorakis from the days of prison camps and exile, who joined him to talk or sing over wine and food until the small hours of the morning.

In Tripolis, when we reached the restaurant after our concert, we found the composer seated with a group of men singing religious music. He waved at me:

"This is where I learned to sing. I sang in the church choir with these men. Listen. You won't hear me sing this sort of thing again."

I knew that Theodorakis had spent his adolescent years in this town, one of the most politically conservative towns in Greece. He became a cantor in the church choir and at the age of fourteen wrote one of his first compositions for the choir. He and his friends read Yiannis Ritsos together, and when the Italians occupied the town, he was arrested in a demonstration. It was his first experience of torture.

I turned my attention to this group of middle-aged men in dark suits. They were concentrating on the music, solemnly singing a hymn from the Orthodox Church service. Mikis's strange, breathy voice blended surprisingly smoothly into the ensemble. I had never seen him look happier. His face was slightly flushed and when they finished he beamed and nodded at me again.

"Beautiful, eh?"

"Beautiful," I replied, raising my glass to the singers.

I was curious about the man opposite me and what he was doing at this table. His black hair was neat and graying. A thin moustache framed his mouth and he wore a dark silk tie. He didn't join in the singing. I asked him what brought him to the dinner. He was, he told me, a bank manager.

"We were all in prison together," he said, waving an inclusive arm towards the end of the table where Mikis and his friends were singing.

"There weren't many of us on the Left in this town and they knew where to find us. There was no chance to escape, so we waited for them to come and arrest us: Makronissos, Ikaria — I did fourteen years. Andonis there did twelve. Together we've served hundreds of years."

He looked sadly at his plate. Life seemed to have robbed him of the ability to join in the joyful reunion of his singing and drinking comrades. Instead, he changed the subject and courteously asked me about Australia.

The tour took us through some of the most dramatic country in Greece, but no-one paid attention to it. Somewhere on the road to Sparta we stopped at a roadside restaurant beside a canyon of orange stone. A goat was tied up nearby, and we sat under a giant, moss-covered plane-tree near a gushing spring where the taverna-owner filled his water-jug. I sat with the two bouzouki-players and the bass-player. Many Greeks considered Lakis Karnezis to be the greatest bouzouki player in Greece. Playing with Theodorakis gave him limited scope to show what he could do, but he knew I was interested in the rembetika, and we talked about the old stars he had worked with.

The social division between the bouzouki-players and the rest of the group was clear. The bouzouki-players were *laïki mousiki* – popular musicians of the old style. They were big stars, but their followers were a different crowd of people from the fans of Theodorakis. They had nothing in common with the pretty young rock-drummer or the electric guitarist and bass-player that Theodorakis, partly in deference to

Preparing for a concert in Volos Stadium, 1975

his children, had included in his band. Nor did they belong with Farandouri, Theodorakis, or the classically-trained pianist. They retained a quality fast disappearing from Greece: *filotimo*. A combination of pride and generosity, *filotimo* demanded that Lakis, unlike the other musicians, cross the road, make his way to the kitchen and carry my food to the table himself, having paid for it in advance out of his own pocket. We ate wild greens, artichokes, home-made sausage, and cheese washed down with a fine local wine until the bus driver swung himself up the steps of our bus and honked his horn.

Before the concert in Larissa, Theodorakis took the microphone: "In 1965 we tried to hold a concert here but the police wouldn't allow it," he said when the cheering had died down. "Then we tried to use an outdoor cinema. Again the police refused permission because they said it was outside and they might not be able to control the crowd. That was at eleven in the morning. So we whistled. And by two in the afternoon, there was a fence right round the cinema. Back to the police station again. This time we got permission and the concert was packed. We started the concert but then we heard planes overhead. We looked up and we saw Air Force planes flying right above us. This went on all night, drowning out the music. So now I'm back in Larissa, and this time you'll have your concert."

Theodorakis conducting his work in Greece at a concert in 1975.

The crowd roared as Mikis brought down his right arm and the concert began. That night, or perhaps the next — by now the nights were merging into one —, we were struck by a plague of locusts. At least that was what I imagined a plague of locusts to be like. Exactly what sort of insects they were I never discovered. Four inches long with fat, grub-like bodies, they began dropping onto us as we played. Everyone swatted them away, and soon there was a mixture of revulsion and hilarity as some musicians stood up and tried to stamp on the insects and others ducked. Theodorakis, who could see the concert was teetering on the brink of collapse, began swatting insects in time to the music as he conducted. We were not only delighted by his performance, which the audience couldn't see, but ashamed of our panic and the concert went on.

I understood, as I had never understood before, Mikis's ability to lead in a crisis, something I'd heard about often, and sensed through his music, but not experienced first-hand. Theodorakis was not always successful in politics, and he was often criticized for his statements, but when people came into direct contact with him they were unable to resist his combination of serious purpose and humor. I watched him from the back of the stage smiling encouragement at us and flinging fat insects to one side with each wave of his arms and I knew I would have followed him unquestioningly into the thick of battle.

6. Thanassis

We were both a little nervous that first night. Thanassis knew he was on show - an exhibit from the colorful past of Greek music - and I was embarrassed to ask him questions in case I looked like a reporter from some travel magazine seeking out interesting characters.

The times Thanassis grew up in were amongst the most troubled in Greece's troubled history and he lived at the eye of the storm. In 1920 the Greek army invaded the hinterland of Smyrna in a fit of grandiose ambition, hoping to realize a dream that had sustained them through years of Ottoman rule: the recapture of Constantinople. The campaign ended not only in the complete defeat of the Greek forces by the Turkish army led by a young Kemal Ataturk, but in the burning of most of the city of Smyrna. The destruction of Smyrna is known simply as "The Catastrophe" in Greek, as much for the loss of the war as for its aftermath.

Under the terms of the international peace agreement that followed the war, all Christians living in Turkey were declared to be Greek and repatriated to Greece. All Muslims living in Greece were also declared Turkish and sent back to Turkey. This draconian arrangement, which had little to do with the complicated realities of life and family alliances in late Ottoman society, caused a human upheaval of unimaginable proportions. Nearly a million Christian refugees flooded into Greece, adding to the half million who had fled Turkey before the war. The population of the young Greek state before the influx was only about four and a half million. The majority were peasants working small plots of land scattered throughout the mountainous mainland and the many islands of the archipelago. There was virtually no industry or infrastructure to deal with the flood of refugees from Smyrna and the surrounding area, and despite some state-enforced resettlement in northern Greece, there was little unoccupied arable land to give them. In tents and makeshift hovels, the Asia Minor refugees competed with the poor of Piraeus and Athens for whatever work and food was available. They had the advantage of coming from a more sophisticated urban society and many of them would eventually make their way into the Greek middle class, but at the time when Thanassis was a boy, they were as penniless as he.

Had it not been for the refugees, the music called rembetika would probably not have become the basis of Greek popular music. The rembetika are songs that like the blues, flamenco, and tango, began at the bottom of society and worked their way to the top; they owe their first flourishing to the creative cross-breeding brought about by migration and poverty and yet they eventually become a source of national identity and pride.

In the cosmopolitan cities of the late Ottoman Empire like Smyrna, you could hear classical and popular Turkish music, the latest European dance music, Romanian and Slavic music, Armenian music, and the Ladino songs of the Jewish community. The refugee musicians who poured into Greece were accomplished in most of these styles, and began playing in cafés much like those they had left behind in Asia Minor. Known as *cafés aman*, these clubs were frequented by refugees and by the lower classes of Athens. Usually there was a male or female singer accompanied by a trio or quartet of instruments such as the violin, santouri, oud, kanun, and guitar. The musicians would perform the music popular in Smyrna and Istanbul, singing mostly in Greek but sometimes in Turkish. Among their songs would always be a few more risqué lyrics about the underworld or the smoking of hashish.

To listen to the songs, visit goo.gl/yjDoyj

Η φωνή του αργιλέ

Πέντε χρόνια δικασμένος μέσα στο Γεντί Κουλέ
από το πολύ σεκλέτι το `ριξα στον αργιλέ
Φύσα, ρούφα, τράβα τονε, πάτα τονε κι άναφτονε
Φύλα τσίλιες για τους βλάχους, κείνους τους δεσμοφυλάκους

Κι άλλα πέντε ξεχασμένος από σένανε καλέ
για παρηγοριά οι μάγκες μου πατούσαν αργιλέ
Φύσα, ρούφα, τράβα τονε, πάτα τονε κι άναφτονε
Φύλα τσίλιες για τους βλάχους, κείνους τους δεσμοφυλάκους

Τώρα που `χω ξεμπουκάρει μέσα απ' το Γεντί κουλέ
γέμωσε τον αργιλέ μας να φουμάρουμε καλέ
Φύσα, ρούφα, τράβα τονε, πάτα τονε κι άναφτονε
Φύλα τσίλιες για τ' αλάνι κι έρχονται δυο πολιτσμάνοι

The Voice of the Hookah

Five years I got in Yendi Koule jail,
ball and chain turned me on to the hookah.
Blow it, suck it, draw it back, turn on and light it up.
Keep watch for those dummies, the dreaded prison guards.

And another five years forgotten by you,
for comfort the manghes *who smoked the hookah,*
Blow it, suck it, draw it back, turn on and light it up.
Keep watch for those dummies, the dreaded prison guards.

Now I'm outside, out of Yendi Koule
fill up my pipe and let's smoke it, man.
Blow it, suck it, draw it back, turn on and it light up.
Keep a watch for the bum, here come two rotten cops.

The songs also talked about the pleasure of sharing the *arghilé* or wa-ter-pipe. Smoking hashish was common in the late Ottoman times, and seems not to have been prosecuted in Greece before the 1930's. This didn't mean that it was condoned in polite society, especially Greek Christian society. It was associated with the music that would later be called rembetika and with the poor neighborhoods near the port of Piraeus, where the refugees had taken up temporary residence in box-cars, tents and shanties alongside Greek dock-workers, shipbuilders, fishmongers, and members of the underworld. Here, refugee musicians and local Greeks played music together and smoked hashish in shacks known as *tekedhes*. Here, too, an instrument called the bouzouki was suddenly all the rage, subsuming all the instruments of the café aman, and becoming as closely identified with these low-down songs as the guitar is with flamenco.

By the time Thanassis was seventeen he was working with his boat-building uncles by day and listening to the sound of the bouzouki by night. The bouzouki had already become fashionable in Piraeus, and Thanassis bought a cheap instrument, teaching himself a handful of songs. He found two neighbors who played a little and together the three young men began earning a few drachmas in the evenings at waterfront cafés. Somehow he survived the famine that killed almost a million Greeks that first winter of the German Occupation. He watched the children of his neighborhood grow hairy with malnutrition, and saw the dead collected each morning from the street. Whenever he had any spare food he gave it away, but first, he managed to eat.

"People ate nettles in those days, and they swelled up and died. Me, I was smart. I collected pieces of wood. We made a little boat, then we waited for customers to buy it. But what were they going to pay us in, thousand drachma notes? The bills were as worthless as lettuce leaves. What we wanted was oil, a handful of flour. We traded our boat for food."

There were two great pleasures in Thanassis' life: music and "the black stuff." In the summer of 1943, he began performing with a legendary rembetika musician named Yorgos Batis. They would play together for four years. What Thanassis liked best about Batis was his sense of humor:

"That guy was so funny, he'd make us make laugh when we were supposed to be playing and we'd have to stop. No-one could go on when Batis started to clown around. We used to get high together, take a fishing-boat and sail it out to sea. Batis would take his baglama, and we'd play music and sing, eat, sleep, and start over again next morning – smoking, eating, making music. What a life!"

"That Batis, he loved to smoke. Before they were all famous, he went on tour with Markos, Artemis and Stratos. And they turned up on Zakinthos. You know the sort of songs they have on the island of Zakinthos, those Italian-style serenades. They'd never heard the rembetika and they didn't like the bouzouki. So the musicians weren't doing well, singing in some dump opposite a café where there was a group with guitars singing the local stuff. Soon all the money was gone and they didn't even have their boat-fare back to Athens. So Batis thinks up a plan. They borrow some dark suits and a couple of black bags, and they head out into the countryside. Batis arrives at a farm and says to the farmer: 'I understand there are some sick animals on your farm. We're veterinarians from Athens and we've come to treat them.'

"The farmer scratches his head. 'Not me,' he says, 'I haven't got any sick animals, but my brother-in-law in the next village, he's got a sick donkey. Won't get up on its feet.'

"Now this is bad," says Thanassis, "because the man's poor and he's only got one donkey. If the donkey won't get up, he can't do anything. So Batis goes to the brother-in-law's house and tells him the same story. The man's a bit suspicious, but he tells him the donkey's really sick."

"'Just you leave him to me,' says Batis, 'but I'll have to be alone with the donkey for half an hour.'"

"Batis has brought his pipe along and the last of the good hashish they've brought from Piraeus and they light up beside the donkey. Each time one of them takes a puff they blow the smoke carefully into the donkey's nostrils. After a while the donkey's ears begin to prick up and in a few minutes it's on its feet, stoned out of its brain and galloping around the paddock. The owner comes out and stares at the donkey in amazement.

'You fixed him all right,' he says. 'What medicine did you give him?'

'It's a new drug from Athens,' says Batis, winking at the boys.

'How much do I owe you for the treatment?'

'That'll be three hundred drachmas,' says Batis, after a quick bit of mental arithmetic.

"The farmer pays up – he's so glad to have his donkey on its feet.

'Let's split fast and get the first boat to Athens,' says Batis, 'before that donkey comes down.'

"Ah," says Thanassis, wiping his eyes, "That Batis! Quite a comedian."

My conversations with Thanassis formed the backbone of my book on the rembetika. I felt as if I had been led to him by amazing luck and that sitting at his feet to listen to his stories was as good an education as I could ever have about the music of the Piraeus underworld. I visited other musicians to talk about their lives, but Thanassis was scornful of most of them. To him they had all sold out.

"Po, po!" he would say, shaking one hand as if he had set it down on a rotten fish. "You wouldn't want to meet him on a dark night!"

He hoped I would write the story of his life, but I had set out to write about the music and he would have to make do with his role as my star informant. By the time I got around to writing about his life, Thanassis would be long dead.

Dress was important to Thanassis as it was to all the Greeks who played bouzouki music. At home on the island he wore a singlet in summer, an old sweater in winter, but when he went down to the port, he would never fail to put on a jacket and a hat. As it was for the musicians who played jazz and blues in the cities of the US, or the stars of the London music halls, dress was a measure of success. The musicians of Thanassis' milieu favored broad brimmed "Republican" hats, pointed, two-tone shoes, and sharp suits. Overcoats were long and worn draped on the shoulders, mafia style.

Thanassis

Thanassis was delighted to see his picture in my book not once but three times. He had reveled in hamming for the photographer and rightly regarded it as book largely devoted to him. The book would bring him visitors, customers for his instruments, pupils who wanted to learn the bouzouki or guitar from him. When the book was translated into German, Thanassis agreed to come with me and a group of older musicians on a tour to promote it. He knew so much more than I did about the ways of old Greek musicians, and when he set eyes on the ones we were going to Germany with, he made his usual gesture of shaking a bad fish smell from his hand. If I had listened to him we probably would never have gone, but by then there were concerts organized in Germany and a publisher waiting to meet us. Besides, Thanassis had an ulterior motive. He wanted to buy a hat.

7. Bouzoukis in Berlin

Renate, the German publisher,wanted musicians who had played with the old-timers, and who would look and sound like authentic rembetes. I found three musicians who had successful careers in Greece, but I was determined to take Thanassis too.

I had warned the musicians that they would be paid very little, but a free trip to Germany appealed to them, even on Syrian Airlines. Thanassis refused to fly.

"Po, po! I've never been on one of those aeroplanes, Kid, and I'm not going to get on one now. Don't you worry about me. I'll be nice and cozy on the train."

"But you'll be all by yourself, and when you leave Greece you won't know the language."

"I know English," he said, "Everyone'll speak English. You just be there at the station to meet me, and I'll be fine."

I always wondered how Thanassis had survived in New York with his meager, mangled English. Would he manage on a German train?

Before Thanassis left, he came into Athens and we met the musicians in a café near Monastiraki Station. I looked sideways at the lead bouzouki-player, Spyros K., a suavely suited man in tinted glasses who had made a fortune in the days when good bouzouki-players were showered with money. He exuded confidence and cologne. I decided he must be down on his luck if he'd agreed to come on this tour. Next to him sat Panos Petsas, who played the guitar, and a miniature version of the bouzouki. I had him to thank for the other two players since we had played together in Theodorakis' band.

Petsas was wearing a plaid tamoshanter and a short gabardine rain-coat, both of which seemed to be aimed at making him look youthful, but only succeeded in making him look like an elderly tourist. When he smiled he displayed dazzling dentures while his eyes stayed cool as two black buttons behind his gold-rimmed glasses. The third member of the trio, Koulis Skarpelis, had a long thin moustache that stretched his cat-like smile almost to his ears.

Thanassis nudged me in the ribs and whispered in my ear, "Where did you find this lot? Mafiosi, all of them. Just watch out, or they'll skin you alive."

After he had left for the railway station I agreed to meet the other three musicians at the airport next day and went home to bed. What was I doing, I thought, taking these three aging and suspicious-looking musicians to Berlin? I'd never been to Berlin myself, nor met my German translator and publisher. What would I do if Thanassis didn't turn up? These men could play the music, I knew, but Thanassis didn't trust them, and besides they were strangers, and Thanassis was a friend. How had I got myself into such a crazy situation? Besides, I was afraid of many things, including flying.

When we arrived we were reassured by Renate. She was a strikingly attractive woman with a round head and dark hair cut very short who hugged us all and swept us off in a taxi to her apartment. Conversation was awkward, with me translating and the musicians looking around in some surprise at the spare white apartment, with its complete absence of Greek sofas and bric-a-brac. Tea was served in plain white cups with dark bread and cheese. Spyros K. managed some words of German and English. The other two spoke to one another in Greek. They were already suspicious, discontented and dying to go shopping. I was anxious about Thanassis, who was to arrive at the railway station in half an hour. I left them in the apartment to fend for themselves while I went to meet him.

Thanassis looked old, tired and triumphant as he got out of the train with his suitcase and his bouzouki-case. I was so pleased to see him that I nearly wept. I brought him back to Renate's apartment, and he immediately charmed her without any linguistic help. By now the musicians were fed up and insisted we go straight to the hotel. When I told Renate, she said she had a wonderful surprise for them, but first we would have to go by the Bethanien Center and meet the man who had organized the Berlin concert.

Complaining noisily in Greek, the musicians climbed into a taxi with me while Renate took Thanassis in another. We headed for Bethanien, an area of Berlin where many of the "guest" workers lived and where the German government had recently built a center designed to meet the cultural needs of these workers by arranging concerts, showing films, and organizing exhibitions. The director, Herr F, greeted us effusively. He was genuinely interested in Greeks, he told me. He'd been to Greece on holidays and loved Greek music. By this time the three professional musicians were ready to mutiny. They had one thing in mind: to get to their hotel, dump their luggage and get to the shops. I asked Herr F. if we could go to the hotel soon because the musicians were tired from their journey.

Again we climbed into taxis, and headed away from the lively, crowded streets around the Bethanien Center. To the musicians' dismay, we were now entering what looked like a small forest. "Where are they taking us?" asked Petsas. "To the countryside?"

We stopped at a group of buildings set in amongst the trees of a small city park. Here was our lovely surprise: a group of elegant Bauhaus-style studios reserved for visiting artists to Berlin.

Spyros, Koulis and Petsas looked even more unhappy when they saw the bare interior of the studios with divan beds on raised platforms leaving maximum floor-space for painters or cellists to practice their art. Herr F., his pink and pleasant face shining, gave me a run-down of the luminaries who had slept in the studios… Chagall, Casals, Ionesco…"

Spyros called me aside.

"Look," he said, "They may think we're old musicians who don't know any better, but if they think we're going to stay in a *han*, they've made a mistake. I wouldn't expect a camel-driver to stay here."

I was getting rather fed up with the stream of complaints.

"They're doing us a real honor. It's just a style of architecture you're not used to. It was designed by a famous architect and all sorts of famous people have stayed here."

"There's no way I'm staying here," said Petsas, pursing his lips. "They think they can have us on the cheap, but they're wrong. We're not asking for a first class hotel. Just somewhere comfortable downtown."

Thanassis didn't say a word.

By now Herr F. and Renate could see that something was wrong. How was I going to explain to them that the musicians refused to stay in a studio designed by Walter Gropius?

"The musicians don't want to stay here," I told them. "They're not used to a place like this. They want to go to an ordinary hotel downtown."

Herr F.'s cheeks went a darker shade of pink.

"But we did this as a great honor to them. It took me a lot of trouble to arrange. Tell them they must stay here... tell them...that Samuel Beckett slept here!"

I was too upset to laugh. Instead of translating his remarks, I told the musicians it would be a great insult not to take the studios that had been arranged for them.

"Ask him what I'm supposed to do if I want a woman in the night," said the 70 year-old Petsas snappily. "We'll pay extra for the hotel ourselves...anything but sleep in this dump."

Again I avoided direct translation, and told Herr F. the musicians were prepared to pay for a hotel themselves rather than sleep in the studios.

The three musicians stood their ground, and Herr F. was forced to back down. We got into a cab and headed downtown until we found some rooms in a second-rate hotel. Judging by the girls walking by,

Petsas would not have far to go if he needed some cheer in the night.

I felt depressed about the whole idea of coming to Germany, and guilty about having persuaded Thanassis that he would have fun in Berlin. I was furious with the three other musicians and embarrassed for my German hosts. By next morning, to my surprise, everyone was happy. The trio were warming up to being on tour, and delighted that they had won a victory over their hosts by being moved from a dump fit for camel-drivers to a decent hotel.

Trouble began again just before the concert. The musicians were hoping, Petsas informed me, to score a little *mavraki* before they played. That was one reason they'd come, he reminded me. Things were getting so difficult in Athens, with all the foreign hippies. This time Thanassis was on their side. The thought of performing with nothing to put them in the mood….

Finding them a hotel was one thing, I told him, but where was I going to find some dope in a strange city? Maybe tomorrow, I suggested, and the concert went on, but it was a strangely solemn affair until Thanassis picked up one of his little baglamas and began singing in a gravely voice. The crowd fell for him immediately as he warmed to his role as an underworld character, clowning shamelessly, rolling his eyes and making asides in heavy underworld slang that delighted the Greeks in the audience. Even Petsas was in high spirits.

Thanassis muttered about how much better he would have been if he'd found something to smoke first, but he knew he'd been the star of the evening and dug me in the ribs now and then, winking in the direction of the "professionals."

"We showed them, Kid. Didn't think I had the chops, but we showed them."

The next concert was in Wupperthal. At least I knew someone there. P., a jazz bass-player who had organized the concert, was a frequent visitor to Athens. He probably knew where to acquire what the musicians needed to get in the mood for the performance. As the train sped through the Berlin corridor I gazed out the window at the spring landscape and half-listened to the musicians talking. Not having found anything to smoke the night before, their conversation turned to the pleasures of the smoking and women. Petsas was telling a long story about playing in a band in Alexandria, and how an Arab had approached him at the club and offered him a job. The man took Petsas on a long drive into the desert and stopped at a small shack, where he was offered a *narghilé*. What happened afterwards involved music, hashish of mythical quality and women to match, with Petsas the center of attraction, charming the Arabs with his music. Thanassis went on to tell a story about how he used to hide his hashish in the basement of his "Green" Village apartment. It was laced with honey and must have appealed to his German girlfriend's poodle. His description of the dog's behavior when stoned was accompanying by graphic imitations that had the other three musicians weeping.

"Poor dog," said Thanassis, suddenly serious as he finished his tale. "It died the next day."

I was distracted by my first sight of a pheasant beside the train-line, its long golden tail-feathers catching the sun. When I tuned into the conversation again, Spyros K. was talking about the days when bouzouki-players were kings, and the king, who was then the Crown Prince, courted bouzouki-players. Constantine had a ski lodge on top of Mount Parnis. He would send a car to pick up the most famous bouzouki players and singers after they finished work at their clubs and bring them up to entertain him and his friends.

"One night I'm standing on the corner of Syntagma Square with my bouzouki in my hand," Spyros was saying, "and a big black car drives up.

"'You want to make 500 drachmas tonight?' the driver says.

" 'What do I have to do?'

" 'Just play your music and keep you mouth shut,' says the driver.

" So we drive up to the mountain, and there's not another car on the road, and we turn into this place that's hidden away in the pines, and when we go in you can't imagine who's there. There's Vicky Moscholiou and Zambetas! They say Bithikotsis went there one night but they didn't invite him again because he said to the Prince, 'Hey Kostas, how's your mother going?"

"So we play and sing and there's wine and dancing and we leave when the sun's coming up. When the driver drops me off he says. 'One word of this gets out and you're dead!'"

For the rest of the trip we doze. It's late afternoon and already getting dark when we arrive in Wupperthal. P. is waiting on the platform. He is a tall, bear-like man who speaks some Greek and the musicians recognize they are dealing with a musician, the sort who can find them what they want. I am enlisted to persuade him that they really need something to warm them up before they begin. P. says he'll do his best and disappears.

The concert is to be held in a large gothic church. Kostas, who has hardly opened his long, cat-like mouth all day says:

"Could you imagine that we'd ever be playing rembetika in a church? We'd better sing 'The Litany'."

Skarpelis was referring to a song by Tsitsanis about a mangas who goes into the Church of St. Mamas to smoke some hashish. When he lights up, the archangel appears, having inhaled the smoke:

Μου λέει, «Ακου, χριστιανέ, δεν είναι αμαρτία
που μπήκες μες στην εκκλησιά να κάνεις λιτανεία.»

Μα ξάφνου κι ένας καλόγερος μου λέει, «Τράβα πίσω,
Γιατί κι εγώ έχω σειρά καμιά για να ρουφίξω.»

'Christian,' he says, 'it's not a sin
that you've come to perform the liturgy.'

But suddenly a monk appears: 'Get in line,
he tells him, 'It's my turn for a drag!'

Ten minutes before the concert begins there is still no sign of P. The audience is mostly Greek, with a sprinkling of young Germans. The Greeks look uncomfortable on their hard pews in the cold, echoing space, and we are shivering in the vestry. The musicians are gloomy until P. comes in, beaming and out of breath:

"Sorry, it took me a while," he says, handing out a couple of joints.

Thanassis rolls his eyes.

"Praise the Lord!" he says fer- vently, taking a long toke. "We'll give them some music to remem- ber tonight."

This time the musicians were mellow but the audience was dead. It wasn't the sort of ambience where they could dance or sing. They listened in silence, smiling at Thanassis' occasional antics before filing out into the quiet streets. The

Thanassis and I meet with musicians in a café in Monastiraki. L to R, Thanassis, Koulis Skarpelis, Spyros Kalfopoulos, Panos Petsas.

effects of the *mavraki* had worn off and the musicians were all feeling flat. P. asked if they would play a few songs next day at a new bar that was opening in town. There was no money to pay them but the food and wine would be good.

By now, as Thanassis informed me, there was a row going on about money. The three "*mafiosi*" were sure I was being paid a lot of money and pocketing most of it. Why should they play for nothing at a bar? Since I wasn't being paid at all on the tour, I was annoyed with them and decided I would take Thanassis and leave them to grouch in their rooms. But next morning when I met Thanassis they were all waiting with their instruments in the lobby and we set off in several cars for the bar.

It was a cozy, low-ceilinged room, completely filled with young Germans. Chairs were set out for the musicians in a semi circle and they were asked if they would play a couple of songs before we all started to eat lunch. Spyros, who had now assumed the leadership of the group, nodded, and they began a Tsitsanis song. After they had been playing for a minute or so a young, bearded man wandered over to them. He was smoking a large curved pipe.

"Do you smell what I smell?" Thanassis whispered to me. The young man walked over to Koulis and handed him the pipe. Koulis looked at him in amazement, lifted one hand off his bouzouki, and took a long pull. The man solemnly took it back and handed it to Petsas, who smiled for the first time that day. There wasn't a break in the music. After several rounds, Petsas, who had exchanged his ridiculous tamoshanter for a small-brimmed German hat with a feather in it, began to turn his hat around. Even Kalfopoulos gave his bouzouki a few twirls. Thanassis, half in earnest, said: "Boys, do you think we died and went to paradise?"

Thanassis and I had decided not to travel back to Berlin with the other musicians but to stay on by ourselves for a night in Wupperthal.

"Good riddance," he said, as their train pulled out. "Now we're going shopping. You're going to help me buy a hat."

Thanassis was very fussy about hats. He still wore the ones he had bought in New York before he returned to Greece. In winter he wore a Borsalino fedora with a wide brim and in summer, a panama with a black band. He couldn't find the sort of hats he liked on his trips to Piraeus, and this was an opportunity to find just the right hat. Besides, he had been paid for his concerts and he was flush with money.

The shop we found was just what Thanassis had dreamed of. An old-fashioned hat store stocked to the ceiling with European hats. My German was not up to describing the kind of hat Thanassis wanted, but he had no problem. He pointed to a pile of Borsalinos that Al Capone would have been proud to wear and began trying them on. He decided to buy two, one olive green, the other brown.

"Choose yourself a hat, Kid," he said to me.

My eye fell on a black felt hat with a brim almost as wide as Thanassis' and I tried it on. "It suits you," he said and we left the shop with our three hats.

We walked out into the damp gray street, Thanassis dapper in his long overcoat and new olive fedora, me in a long black cloak and my black hat. I twirled around and around, my hat pulled low, my cloak and hair swinging wide in the empty street, giddy with relief that the tour of Germany was over.

"Kid," said Thanassis, laughing, "You look like a beautiful black crow!"

8. Castrato Tenoros, What the Grocer Said, and Some Thoughts on Greek Dancing.

In the winter of 1976 a letter arrived from Paris. It was from Hartley Newnham, an old friend and Australia's leading counter tenor. Would I like to do a concert with him in Athens? He was on his way to sing Monteverdi in Vienna. After that he would like to come to Greece. The Australian Embassy would, he assured me, cover all the costs. If I could play the pieces that suited a harpsichord, a pianist friend would join us to play the piano for some 19th century songs. I was flattered, but as I told Hartley, the troublesome spinet I had played with Theodorakis I had sold, and my own small virginal was somewhere on the high seas between Australia and Greece and I knew no-one else in Athens who had one. Hartley replied that the Australian Embassy would track one down for me.

After a few phone-calls, someone remembered hearing a harpsichord at a concert in the Goethe Institute in Athens. I should try them. A snooty secretary answered my call and had no idea of such an instrument being in the building but she would make inquiries. Her inquiries turned up a long-unused harpsichord stowed in the basement of the Institute. Being an Embassy affair, they couldn't refuse to lend it to me, but, as the secretary reminded me more than once, that didn't include any practice time. It would be brought up from the basement, delivered to the British Council in Kolonaki Square and tuned on the day of the concert. That was all the access I could have to it: one day's worth.

Hartley wrote to say he would arrive two weeks before the concert. Somehow we had to find a place to rehearse, and before then I had to find a keyboard. I panicked and nearly called the concert off, but I had reckoned without Hartley's charm. He looked like most people's idea of an angel. His blond curls framed his handsome, smiling face, and he spoke in a deep, melodious voice. No sooner was he in Athens than things began to happen. An architect and his German wife lent us their piano to practice on, and encouraged us to use it whenever we wished. Hartley had not only brought me music by Dowland, Frescobaldi, and Purcell; he decided he would learn some songs of Theodorakis. We rehearsed for a couple of hours every day, and the rest of the time we were free to explore Athens together. I took him to the hidden tavernas of Athens and out to Aigina to meet my friends. For Hartley, the concert was a breeze. I put off thinking about it too much and tried to enjoy the rehearsals. Then came the question of a press conference. The Embassy wanted to publicize the concert, and had organized a conference at the British Council two days before the concert. Would I interpret?

The press conference turned into a peculiarly Greek fiasco. The first question a reporter asked Hartley was whether 'counter tenor' meant he was a castrato. Greeks were familiar with the idea of castrated singers. Long after the practice had ceased in Europe, the Ottomans castrated men to guard the harem of the sultan. Some may have been castrated to preserve their voices. In any case it was a sufficiently common practice in the Empire that recordings were made of the last surviving castrati. Since the term 'counter tenor' meant nothing to the reporters, they were convinced Hartley must be a castrato. Hartley replied that not only had he not been castrated, but unlike some counter tenors, he didn't have a naturally high singing voice; he had simply discovered that he could sing falsetto and that his high register was more interesting than his low. His answer disappointed the Greek reporters, who had turned up in large numbers and wanted something more exciting to write about than a man who could sing in a high voice. The next day, one of the leading dailies came out with a headline: '*Castrato Tenoros* to Sing at the British Council this Saturday Night.'

"Hell," said Hartley. "I'll have to do something about this or my reputation will be ruined."

The headline had one good result. The auditorium was filled to overflowing. The British pianist Nicholas Routley had arrived from England just in time, making me even more nervous by rippling effortlessly through some Wolf songs with Hartley for an hour before the concert. The harpsichord, as I had been led to expect by the Goethe Society's unhelpful secretary, arrived only an hour before we were to begin. Apart from the curious Athenians, a lot of my friends were in the audience. As the lights went down I cursed myself for my reckless addiction to adventure. The concert had the potential for serious embarrassment.

It was probably due to Hartley's charm that it wasn't. After the early music section I was able to appreciate the extraordinary range of his voice as he sang HugoWolf, John Cage, and Michael Tippet. When we began the Theodorakis songs there was a gasp from the audience. This curious phenomenon was about to sing in Greek! The applause was deafening. Then Hartley called for silence and asked me to translate what he was about to say: "This final song is to establish the fact that I am not a *castrato tenoros*."

I moved to the piano and began the dramatic zeibekiko introduction to the Theodorakis-Ritsos song "On these marbles." The song was a stirring hymn of resistance to the dictatorship. Ritsos had written the lyrics on the island of Samos where he was exiled by the junta. He had managed to send the short poem to Theodorakis in exile as part of a cycle he called *Eighteen Little Songs for the Bitter Homeland*. There wasn't a Greek in the audience who wasn't familiar with the song. An excited murmur rippled around the hall as Hartley began in a deep baritone:

Σε τούτα εδώ τα μάρμαρα κακιά σκουριά δεν πιάνει
μηδέ αλυσίδα στου Ρωμιού και στ' αγεριού το πόδι

On these marbles evil rust can take no hold
nor on the chains of the Greeks, nor the wind's foot.

Εδώ το φως εδώ ο γιαλός χρυσές γαλάζιες γλώσσες
στα βράχια ελάφια πελεκάν τα σίδερα μασάνε

Here the light, here shore – gold, azure tongues —,
on the rocks deer chip away, they eat the iron shackles.

The first lines were drowned in a storm of cheering. Hartley had salvaged his reputation. He was clearly not a castrato. And he had done it with a song that defined the ethos of the Greek Left, the *Romiossini* that bowed but didn't break under oppression. He bowed, serene and triumphant, while my friends headed towards the bar.

Those were the days when wine flowed but hard liquor was heavily taxed. Since my friends were all poor, the sight of a well-stocked bar was irresistible. The Jamaican bar-tender hired for the night soon had their measure. With an indulgent smile he poured serious quantities of bourbon, Scotch and Vodka into them until the bar closed down. One American friend was found semi-conscious on the stairs. Others, like Katerina, had to be helped into the street by their less tipsy partners. All of them had massive hangovers. The concert was, they assured me, a sensation.

*　　*　　*

Before Hartley left Athens the owners of the piano we had practiced on, who had become our friends, suggested we go to a Cretan taverna together. Perfect, I said. I loved Cretan music and dance and I wanted Hartley to see it.

We set out with our hosts and a group of their friends. I found myself sitting next to a man who told me he owned a grocer's shop in Athens. He seemed to know a lot about Greek music, and we were both soon engrossed in the sound of the Cretan lyra, the harsh voice of the singer, the fast-flying feet of the dancers. The lyra is not, as the name suggests, a lyre, but a rebec, a small fiddle played upright, the point balanced on the knee, the strings stopped with the backs of the finger-nails. It is accompanied by a large folk lute that doesn't do much more than keep the rhythm. The dances of Crete are among the most dramatic in the Greek repertoire. The drama is heightened by the traditional Cretan costume, which consists of breeches, (the baggy kind once worn throughout the Ottoman world and later trimmed to the shape of a jodhpur), long black boots, or on festive occasions white, a black shirt, sometimes worn with an embroidered vest, and a crocheted black headband worn low on the brow like a pirate's. A thick black moustache completes the ensemble. Never mind what the women wear; they are completely eclipsed by the men.

The jewel of Cretan dances is not the fast *sousta* or the dramatic *pendozali*, both of which are exhausting and showy, but the *syrtos*. This is where the lyra-player and the dancer improvise and interact with each other. The grocer and I watched with delight as the line of dancers, led by a group of young men, began moving off to the right. The boy first in line, whose job it is to improvise, began twisting and leaping like a young goat, keeping his balance by holding the handkerchief of the next dancer in line. Further down the line the older dancers seemed to walk, rather than dance the steps, conserving their energy. Young men took turns to lead, outdoing each other in their graceful leaping and twirling. Then an older man with a grey moustache who had been walking through his steps at the far end of the line moved up to take the lead. To the casual observer it was an anti-climax. The man wore no costume and moved very little. Only the small triangles of his pointed shoes attracted the eye, hovering, delaying, feinting, syncopating, as he flirted with the lyra-player's phrasing.

The grocer's eyes were fixed on the old man as he danced. He turned to me and said softly, "The young men were talking to the birds; the old man is talking to the stars."

When I translated this to Hartley, Hartley was sure I'd made it up. I was flattered but knew I could never have invented such a description any more than I could have danced the old man's dance.

The musicians had begun to play another syrtos, and a young man came over to ask me to join the line. Dancing in such a taverna where musicians are playing is not a spontaneous activity. You don't just get up when the music moves you. The head of a table of patrons pays the musicians for the privilege of dancing with his party of friends and family. If you are not part of that group, it is an honor to be asked to dance with a line of dancers. Since no-one in our group danced, I was delighted to join the line. I felt I was doing rather well, especially when one of the dancers asked what village I was from on the island. When I sat down the grocer let a little air out of my balloon.

"You have taken many of the colors of Greece," he told me, "but not yet the color of the marble column. When you see the marble column dance, then you will have taken the last color."

I took this to mean I was in Greece's thrall but Greece was not yet in mine. As we left the Cretan taverna still high on the music, the dancing and the grocer's conversation, I wondered how Greeks could speak in such high-flown language without sounding corny. I knew the grocer would have an answer.

"What makes Greeks talk in poetry?" I asked him as we said good-bye.

"It's a small miracle," he answered solemnly. "The poet takes a screwdriver and fixes the stars in the universe."

*   *   *

The zeibekiko dancer dances on the edge of the abyss.
                                                    —Tsarouchis

In the days when it was a part of everyone's life, dancing was not only a language but a magical activity, and because it enchanted it was dangerous. Most Greek writers have avoided describing dance. Nikos Kazantzakis was an exception. His *Zorba the Greek* has become a tourist cliché of what Greek dancing is about, but the novel on which the film was based contains the most interesting descriptions of dance that I know of in Greek literature.

Because it takes place in Crete, there is a scene of Cretan dancing. It is Easter. The narrator and Zorba go to watch the locals dancing in the village. A young shepherd, who comes down once a year from the mountains, is leading the dance:

a dark, virile young man of twenty, his thickly downed check not yet touched by the razor, his bare chest a forest of curly hair, he had thrown his head back, his feet beat the ground like wings, every now and then he turned his glance on some young girl and the whites of his eyes gleamed fiercely in the blackness of his face.

Watching the dancer, the narrator feels "happy, afraid." He asks a villager who the young man is. "He's like the archangel, shameless fellow," the man replies, "who takes souls away."

The young man calls out to the lyra-player, "play-up so Death will die!" Leaping high in the air, he plucks the kerchief from his neighbor's head with his boots. The men applaud the feat of precision and agility, but the girls look down in confusion. The young man continues to dance…

without looking at anyone, wild and disciplined, now resting his left hand on his lean, hard hip…fixing his eyes wildly and modestly on the ground.

The dance is interrupted by an old man who tells the crowd, fired by the dance, that the widow, a beauty hated for spurning the son of a powerful figure in the village and sending him mad, has entered the church. The widow is stabbed by the young man's father on the steps of the church.

The dance as a prelude to violent action, including war, is a ritual action common to many societies and cultures, from the Great Plains of the US to the Black Sea. The Kululi people of the New Guinea Highlands burn the dancers in the Gisaro ceremony by thrusting torches into them as they dance. The dancers are said to represent the sorrows of the audience in their songs and dances, causing a tension that is unbearable unless the audience can retaliate. The smashing of plates at the feet of Greek dancers may be a much milder expression of this tension.

The dance that unleashed the violence in *Zorba* is full of apparent contradictions. The young man's dancing is "wild and disciplined," his eyes look "wildly and modestly" at the ground. That contradiction, I soon understood, is what good Greek dancing is about. It must balance two elements: *tapeinotita* — modesty, and *agriada* — a ferocity that can catch fire. The emotion must be kept coiled, denied an easy outlet. Without restraint, the dancer fails, however nimble his feet. The old man in the Cretan taverna had it. That's why he was able to talk to the stars.

Zorba is a stranger in Crete, a Macedonian who has traveled a great deal, and he dances the only solo dance in the Greek repertoire, a *zeibekiko* that comes from the shores of Asia Minor. A man of action, he finds it difficult to communicate with the scholarly narrator of the book until he teaches him to dance: "To hell with paper and pens," he tells his boss, "Now that you're dancing and you're really learning my language, what won't we have to talk about!" A little later he says, "I have a lot to tell you but my tongue won't get around it…So I'll dance it!"

To the narrator, Zorba, dancing alone on the seashore, is like "an old Partisan archangel" …

You'd think he was calling out 'What can you do to me Almighty? You can't do a thing to me, just kill me. Kill me, and I don't give a damn. I've had my revenge, I've said what I want to say. I managed to dance and I don't need you any more.

Several years ago I came across a novel by the Canadian writer Jane Urquart called *Away*, which is set in an Irish immigrant settlement in Canada at the time of the "troubles" in the home country. The heroine, Eileen, like everyone else in the community, is ravished by the dancing of a young visitor called Lanighan. The young man hardly speaks, and yet he is chosen to make a petition on behalf of the community to a visiting Irish political leader. When Eileen asks the Irish captains how the taciturn Lanigan will make his plea, they answer her with some scorn: "Haven't you been watching? He'll dance. It's what he's been practicing here all week…his petition to McGee."

Puzzled, Eileen asks how McGee will know what he is saying.

"A true Irishman always knows what a dancer is saying," they answer her.

The remark would have made perfect sense to Zorba. Dancing was a language he and his generation understood. It depended, for communication, on a shared history, a shared understanding of what the body said.

9. Zorba

On a visit to Melbourne in 1981, I walked into a wine-bar that I used to frequent as a student. It had been transformed from a small dusty shop to a large and elegant bistro, but I recognized the owner's son pouring glasses of red wine behind the bar, and to my surprise, a customer sitting in the same corner he had occupied on a semi-permanent basis before I left Australia. Born in Czechoslovakia, Peter emanated a languid European charm that I had enjoyed when I was a student. I was happy to find such an enduring embodiment of my youth and joined him for a glass of wine. When we had drunk a glass he told me he had discovered my book on the rembetika and passed it on to a friend of his, a documentary film-producer, telling her it would make a great movie.

By the second glass of wine, Peter had made a telephone call and arranged for us to drive to the producer's house and discuss the project. Peter liked attractive women, and the producer turned out to be one. She lived in a grand suburban house, where we sank into deep couches while she fetched some tea. She was already hooked on the project, she told me, mostly because of Peter's enthusiasm. Soon there was talk of financial backing, camera crews, and directors. I listened in mild disbelief, but after the wine I had drunk with Peter I was content to dream. An hour later I left Peter with his pretty friend and drove out to my mother's house. I didn't see either of them again before I left Australia, and when I got back to my new home in Ithaca, New York, I forgot all about the movie.

The following year Z. spent a semester working with a colleague at the Dutch Meteorological Institute near Utrecht. I had looked forward to being in Europe, exploring a new country, but nothing turned out as I'd hoped. The apartment Z.'s colleague found for us was in the attic of an impeccably clean house in a dull commuting suburb. Every second house had a Mercedes parked outside it and public transport was surprisingly hard to find. Z. was picked up and taken to work each day while I stayed alone in the attic translating Greek poetry and trying to write my own, but the moment I sat down to write, the vacuum-cleaner would roar into life and remain vital until lunchtime. I was so infuriated by the racket that seemed to come right up to the attic door that one day I opened the door a crack and peeped out. The landlady was vacuuming the walls of the stairwell.

The only consolation of being in Bilthoven was that it was not far from Utrecht, which had a wonderful musical life. We went to concerts as often as we could, and if we hurried to the bus-stop, we could just catch the last bus back to Bilthoven. We walked a lot in the town and had planned a trip to Amsterdam when I found a letter waiting for me from the film producer. She asked me to call her in Melbourne because she had some good news.

When I reached her she told me she had hired a director and a crew. Could I go to Greece and set up all the musicians and venues for the crew to arrive in Athens in three weeks' time? The crew would not be able to stay more than a week in Greece; time was money. I would have to have everything ready: hotels, itinerary, sites, images. They would simply film what I told them to. It would be my responsibility to find photographs, old documentary footage, people whose English was good enough to interview, preferably famous Greeks. Theodorakis was a must. The producer was excited and pleased with herself.

"We have the top camera crew in Australia," she told me, "and a very experienced director. That's going to cost us an arm and a leg, but it's worth it. We can't pay anyone for appearing in the film."

"This is amazing!" I stammered. "I'll try to be there by the end of the week."

"I've already booked your flight. You leave on Thursday. You have a lot to do," she said and hung up.

I had never worked on a film. I had two weeks to pull all the pieces of a documentary together and I wasn't sure it was possible. The producer didn't know Greece. She had no idea what it would mean to persuade Theodorakis and other luminaries to be at a certain place at certain time, let alone a collection of elderly musicians who weren't getting paid for their time. Everything depended on my friendships, and the chance that people would be pleased to be in a film, even an Australian film. The one person I knew I could count on to play a starring role was Thanassis. I decided to go straight to the island and talk to him.

The day after I flew into Athens I took the ferry-boat to the island. As always, the harbor opened its arms, full of fishing-boats, their names painted on the prow — Nekatarios, Eleni, Maria — to welcome me. At one end of the harbor two fishermen were mending their nets, and a row of horse-drawn cabs stood in the thin shade of the tamarisks. It was the hour of the siesta and the cafes were mostly deserted. I walked from the boat to Thanassis' house, skirting the old cathedral and scattering ravenous, long-eared cats. I raised the knocker shaped like a woman's hand and let it fall just once in case Thanassis was asleep. "Who is it?" he called.

"It's me Thanassis – Gail—Elektra."

"Po, po! Let yourself in kid," he said.

Thanassis hadn't shaved and grey stubble made him look ten years older. He gave me an awkward hug and we sat down on his narrow bed. The house was as full of knick-knacks, instruments and photographs as ever, but a thick layer of dust covered every surface. Thanassis, who rarely slept by day, had been working on a small baglama, smoothing the handle with a long rasp.

"This one's going to be a beauty – a little fellow with a big voice. The gourd I'm using —it's light, see, and the handle's long, so it's easy to play."

"Guess what Thanassis," I blurted out impatiently. "You're going to be a film star!"

Thanassis was not as impressed as I had hoped he would be. He was willing, of course, but he didn't want to play alone. He'd need to find a bouzouki-player he could rely on, not one of those *mafiosi* like we took to Germany. Iordanis would be best, but he hadn't seen him for months. That meant he was probably drinking too much. It would take time to arrange.

Greeks don't like to be rushed, and I was in a hurry. Thanassis was right: we needed months to set up a movie, not weeks. I looked around the cramped little house I had spent so many hours in and tried to imagine a film crew setting up their lights and cameras there. Perhaps it wouldn't look quite so picturesque to them. It would take more than a day to film and I would have to arrange a hotel for the crew on the island. It was off-season and most of the hotels were closed. Thanassis had stuck with me through the tour of Germany. I knew he would do whatever he needed to do to make his section of the film work, but I was asking a lot of him. He was older now, and there wasn't any money in-volved. I began to feel guilty about dragging him into another adventure that might be a burden to him, but there was enough of the performer still in Thanassis to inspire some effort.

"Don't worry, kid," he said, getting out a packet of Drum tobacco and carefully rolling a cigarette. "We'll give them a good show."

Making the film taught me a lot about Greece that I didn't know. Most of the musicians I contacted expected they would be paid large sums for appearing in a documentary, but all of them wanted to appear in a movie. By the time the film crew arrived, I had organized some of the best musicians in Greece to perform for us, including the great Sotiria Bellou, who was singing with Vassilis Tsitsanis in a club on the outskirts of Athens. Tsitsanis himself refused to appear on camera be-cause he said he was too old to look good on film, but with Bellou's help we were able to sneak in some shots of him in his dressing-room. Theodorakis was happy to talk about the rembetika and its links to the lower classes of Greece, and the younger groups of musicians who were performing around Athens had no objection to the lights and cameras that dominated the clubs they worked in. Even Mariza would be in the movie, singing a song by Tsitsanis. Later, when I helped edit the film, I was amazed at the stars we had managed to film, but despite the luminaries it was still Thanassis who stole the show.

Sitting on his rush stool among his instruments as he worked on a baglama, giving a bouzouki lessons to a young man from the island, singing in Panagakis' wine shop with an old bouzouki-player I had never seen before, and who he had probably paid handsomely to come over from Piraeus, Thanassis turned on a stellar performance. The Australian director and film crew knew nothing about Greek music, but they knew a star when they saw one. They trampled through Thanassis' house, setting up their lights, ordering him to walk from room to room as they re-took shots. His patience was tried almost to breaking point but he confined his objections to muttered Greek asides, and conserved his energy for what mattered most to him, the performance in the wine shop. The wine-shop was an impossible site. It was a dark cave with no windows except on the harbor-side where the sun streamed in. Accommodating the large camera-man, his assistant, the director, the musicians, myself, the owner and enough customers to make it looked occupied was already a feat without the lights and cameras. We had forgotten that there had to be enough room for one of the fishermen to dance a zeibekiko, and the small metal tables were shifted a dozen times so that a tiny square of floor could be opened up.

Thanassis was so nervous that he and his bouzouki-playing friend had primed themselves with some of the 'black'. I was worried that they wouldn't be able to play a note if the delays went on any longer. The owner and the few customers who had squeezed into the wine-shop had frozen in the grave attitudes demanded by Greek photographers. The wine-shop, that was usually raucous with chatter and spitting olive oil, had fallen unnaturally silent. Fortunately my American poet friend Phil, who had come to watching the filming, sat down at one of the tables and started cracking jokes. The cameras rolled and everything went more or less as we had planned. Panagakis, the wine-shop owner, raised a shaky forkful of fried greens to his lips, the baglama announced itself in a high-pitched voice, Thanassis hammered his way through a song about a couple of pick-pockets who got caught in the act, his bouzouki-playing friend kept him on track, and Takis the fisherman stood up to dance a fine zeibekiko on a space the size of a beach towel.

When it was over, Thanassis swore he would never make another film, but I could see he was pleased with himself. "Wait till you see yourself," I told him. "You'll be so happy."

Leaving the island next day, I had a serious brush with one of the harbor officials. It was a Sunday afternoon, and Athenians who had come over to the island for the week-end were returning to Athens. The ferry was packed, and despite the fact that most of the crowd had already purchased tickets, the metal gate to the wharf was suddenly lowered. The two camera-men had gone ahead with their heavy equipment, and I was following with the director. Between us and the crew was a barrier manned by a uniformed Greek official who was bearing the fury of a crowd of frustrated passengers with the indifference of his uniformed authority. I had been chatting to the director in English. He was used to pulling strings and was astonished to find himself helpless to get on board with his crew. He told me to explain to the harbor official that we were a group and couldn't be separated because the camera-crew didn't know their way around Athens. I did as I was told, knowing this would get us nowhere. Then I began to worry about what would happen if the camera crew really did get lost in Piraeus. I left my Australian etiquette behind me and turned on a thoroughly Greek performance. I yelled, I let a few tears trickle down my cheeks, I appealed to the crowd for sympathy, and in no time we were through the gate.

As we joined the camera-crew they looked at me in astonishment.

"Struth," said the cameraman, "I didn't think you had it in you!"

This improved my status with the film-crew, who had found me less than satisfactory in arranging the conditions they were used to. The hotel I put them in, for example, was comfortable and had splendid views of the Acropolis, but they demanded one where there was room-service twenty-four hours a day.

I wasn't sorry when the filming was over. I always disliked having anything between me and the music I loved. If I had been a more serious musicologist I could have recorded amazing musical moments over the years I spent with Greek musicians. And if I had carried a camera with me, I could have captured a thousand shots of famous musicians. But I always felt that the camera or the tape-recorder got in the way of relating to musicians. It was a form of collecting, something I had an aversion to. I knew that the camera-men and the director had no idea about what they had filmed. To them it was an assignment, and I had presented it to them as if it belonged to me. It made me feel like an imposter. Now what would they do with it?

The director realized the problem when they got back to Melbourne. Without me, they had very little idea who they had filmed, or what the songs were about. I would simply have to come to Melbourne to help edit the film. The director would write a script with me and we would find a big star to record it.

By the time I reached Australia a lot of the editing was done. It was no use my lamenting the footage that was gone; instead I tried to make sense of what the editor and the director had saved. I realized I had no idea what the camera crew had been doing when they weren't filming musicians. They had disappeared for an hour or two each day to take location shots, and flown to Istanbul on their way home for some background footage. The camerawork was ravishing. The laconic camera-man who had hardly addressed five words to me had turned his loving lens on Greek and Turkish cats, pretty girls, the brilliance of Greek light and the muted grays of Istanbul. The director and I argued about some of the footage and about how to write a script to match it, but by the time I left Melbourne I knew we had a film that was beautiful to look at and had enough of Thanassis in it to keep him and any audience happy.

The director wanted a big name to read the script and he had two people in mind: Melina Mercouri and Anthony Quinn. Melina I could understand, but Quinn wasn't even Greek. Why would we have him narrate the film?

"Look, it doesn't matter what he is. Everyone thinks of him as Zorba the Greek."

Theodorakis had suffered from the "Zorba factor" on his tours. In Australia, his audience had shouted for Zorba until he had shouted back at them:

"I didn't come here to entertain you with Zorba. There's a dictatorship in Greece and all you want is Zorba!"

Now the director wanted Anthony Quinn to narrate a film about rembetika. I balked. I wasn't keen on Melina either. I couldn't see what these big stars would do for the film except add a false sense of glamour to it. The director was adamant.

"Nobody knows a thing about Greek music, and they don't care about authenticity. If we're going to get a broad audience we need a name. See what you can do!" he told me in a tone that indicated he would choose his narrator with or without my help.

It was all very well to use my contacts in Greek music. But how, I wondered, was I going to approach a couple of film stars, especially now that I was back in suburban Holland with my husband.

Melina proved hard to find, so reluctantly I rang Quinn's agent,

William Morris, in New York. The man who answered the phone sounded as incredulous as I felt.

"You want Mr. Quinn to narrate an Australian documentary film about Greek music?" he asked. "You realize Mr. Quinn's fee is $20,000 a day and that is for voice only. It doesn't include an on-camera appearance."

I was relieved. This put Quinn out of the picture. I called the director.

"$20,000" he responded coolly. "It's a bit steep. I wonder if we can bring him down. I tell you what. Find his home address from William Morris and send him a copy of your book with a nice little letter telling him how much you'd like him to do it, how he's everyone's idea of Zorba the Greek, and say you're on a tight budget."

Anthony Quinn, I found out, was in living in Rome with his Italian wife. He also had an apartment in New York. I put the book with its cheap brown paper cover in an envelope with an ingratiating note and sent it off.

Three weeks later the phone rang. It was the same William Morris Agency man who had made me feel like a poor petitioner at court.

"Mr Quinn liked your book," he said crisply, "and he'll do it for half his normal fee."

Again I was sure we were off the hook. To me, $10,000 sounded like a lot of money. The director didn't blink an eye.

"We'll accept. Leave the rest to me. I'll set it up in a studio in New York, but you have to get it done in one day, or we'll be in trouble."

I was happy to leave the arrangements to the director. I was out of my depth, and had no desire to speak to the tough-talking agent at William Morris again. It was enough to have to coach Anthony Quinn for a day.

It was strange to be flown here and there by a film company whose idea of money still seemed to me like a game of Monopoly. I walked into the foyer of the hotel they had booked for me on Central Park South wishing I had something suitable to wear to an appointment with a star. To my surprise no-one had come to meet me. Everything had been negotiated from afar. I was to turn up at 9 a.m. the next morning at a studio downtown where Mr. Quinn would be waiting for me.

Quinn may have looked like everyone's idea of a Greek, an Italian, or an Eskimo, but he worked like an American. The script we had written in Melbourne was much too long, and Quinn didn't care for it, especially the references to drugs. ("When I was in Greece there wasn't any of this talk about drugs," he said to me with obvious distaste). He wanted to improvise, and now and then he did. He also didn't enjoy being told how to pronounce Greek words, especially by a nobody like me. But he worked, and he didn't have to be told anything twice. By the end of the day we were both exhausted, but the script was done.

He looked at me with a mixture of impatience and respect.

"Honey," he said, "You know I got an Oscar for a film where I said seven words!"

The results of our rather unusual collaboration can be seen on the film *Rembetika: the Blues of Greece*, directed by Philippe de Montigny, at goo.gl/Kpd7z2

The zeibekiko still had some dangerous magic to it when I lived in Greece. There was a thin, edgy boy called Loukas who danced with a group of his friends at a tiny bar with a good juke-box in it called "Zoumeli's." I never cared for Loukas or his friends much, but I occasionally put my head in the door just to watch them dance. They were all good dancers, but Loukas danced with a wildness that set him apart. When he had enough money he would go "to the bouzoukis." We went to hear the great rembetika singer Sotiria Bellou one night with Loukas and several friends. He was drinking hard and at some point he smashed his wrists on some broken glass. Self-mutilation was not uncommon in the circles of the early rembetika dancers, but it was new to me. It would cost more than Loukas had in his pocket to pay for the privilege of having the dance floor to himself, but Bellou, who had been watching him, and knew he could dance, called out in her deep contralto: "This one's for Loukas."

Loukas stood up and moved onto the tiny dance-floor. His dancing was low to the ground, with feats of agility that were not as remarkable as the sustained ferocity of his performance. Blood trickled down his arms to the dusty floor, and it seemed to me to be a histrionic display, but Bellou sensed something genuine in the drama of his dancing. She sang for him and he danced for her. It was rare to see such dancing in Athens, where many Greeks regarded the bouzouki clubs as a place to be seen spending large sums of money. This singer, who had spent her life defying the conventions of Greek society, and fought with the partisans in the war, recognized a dancer who bewailed his fate in his zeibekiko. If anyone had dared to step onto the dance-floor when Loukas was dancing, I hate to think what might have happened.

*   *   *

Thanassis had always wanted me to write the story of his life. He would tell it to me in his own words and I would write it down. Each year I promised I would sit with him, each year he promised he would talk into a tape recorder and make me cassettes, each year something got in the way. Eventually he told his story to some young

Thanassis at home

Greeks who studied bouzouki with him and he published it at his own expense, but it was not the book he hoped for, not what we would have written together years earlier, before his world became bitter and small.

Ten years after the documentary film had made Thanassis a star I went to Aigina for a night. Six months earlier I had made what I thought would be my last visit to him. Clearly, he was dying. I was never quite sure how old he was; he avoided questions about his age but he had to be well into his eighties. I had had no news of him since my last visit and I decided to wait until morning to visit the house. That night I woke with an acute attack of food poisoning and spent the hours until morning getting rid of whatever caused it. I felt too sick to visit Thanassis on my way to the port where I took a boat back to Athens. By evening I had recovered, and I planned to go to a concert where Diamanda Galas was performing. I was about to leave Mariza's house for the concert hall when the phone rang. It was Thanassis. Someone had seen me on the waterfront in Aegina, and told him. Why hadn't I come to see him?

I explained as best I could, but Thanassis kept repeating that he must to talk to me; he had something very important to tell me and it was urgent that I come back to the island. I explained I was leaving for America the next day, apologized profusely and hung up. "That was Thanassis," I told Mariza. "He's upset because I was on the island and didn't visit him. I think he's dying."

"Elektra," she said, "you'll probably never see him again. You can always go to a concert, but you can't make things right with Thanassis again. Call the waterfront and see what time the last boat sails."

It was already 7.30 and I wanted to go to the concert very much. I called the harbor. The last boat was the slow ferry. It was leaving at 8.00 and would take two hours to reach Aigina. By that time Thanassis would be in bed. I flew out the door and into the clamorous rush-hour traffic of Athens to hail a cab. I caught the *Ellas* with minutes to spare, and sank onto a bench in the smoke-filled bar feeling exhausted and depressed. I knew what Thanassis would have to say. For years now, his monologue had been entirely predictable:

That bastard up there, (pointing to the heavens). *Last week*

He let the propeller of a hydrofoil chop a boy into pieces. The kid was swimming in the sea, and the propeller just sliced him up. And all the rich people, those filthy crooks who have all the money — they're so greedy, see —- they don't care. All they want is more and more, and they squeeze the lemon, and when there's no juice in the lemon they squeeze it some more; it's all fixed, you see, fixed by the big companies and the fat cats that have taken over the whole world and are destroying it...and when I get up there I'll tell him, that big boss in the sky; I'll say 'what did you do to stop those fat bastards?'....They've written a book about my life — I told them things, but they didn't get it right. You should have written it. You would have told them how I think about life, all the things that are in the songs.

It was after ten when I took the little street that leads from the waterfront to the old cathedral. The streets were quiet and most of the cafés were empty. Behind the cathedral I turned into the lane where Thanassis lived and looked through the iron gate to his courtyard. A light was still burning but there was no response to the electric buzzer on the wall.

"Thanassi!" I called.

"Who is it?"

"It's me."

"Wait!" he croaked in a hoarse voice, "Let yourself in."

I lifted the latch on the sky blue door. The small courtyard, overhung with grapes and jasmine, looked much as usual. I had spent many hours in this house, watching Thanassis shape his instruments: baglamas, bouzoukis,

Thanassis's courtyard on the island of Aigina

tzouras —rasping, polishing, and stringing them as he sat on a small stool, a chipped coffee cup and an ashtray beside him. He would stop work, offer me whatever was in the refrigerator, pick up an instrument and play. Then he would tell me a story or roll himself a joint before taking up his bouzouki again. I was so used to the house, to his camp bed covered by a rough red flokati rug where we sat while he played and I strummed a baglama; it was only when I brought my children to visit him that I realized how squalid it had become, how the whole remarkable collection of instruments and bric-a-brac had accumulated a thick coat of dust, the toilet was filthy, the taps didn't work and the house smelled of urine and mold.

That night as he shuffled to the door in his white cotton vest, I saw a shrunken, yellow old man. The effort of getting to the door had tired him, and he sat fighting for breath on the bed. Then he cleared his throat and spat into a cigarette box. His hands, brown and surprisingly smooth, shook as he labored to roll himself a joint. Between fits of coughing followed by hawking and spitting, he began to talk. The stream of bile that poured from him had changed very little from last year or the year before.

Everything in the world was arranged — the rich, evil people were in charge and they had screwed the rest of us. No-one else realized what was happening but he had worked it all out, and when he got up there he would tell that bastard in the sky that he was responsible for all the evil in this life, and on and on, and on until I wondered why I had come. It was difficult to see behind this embittered remnant of a man the funny, charming musician, the graceful dancer, the man in whose company I had once felt so comfortable.

I listened for as long as Thanassis had breath, took his frail body in my arms and left. Two months later he died. A friend sent me photographs of the empty courtyard with its sky blue doors and shutters closed, a half-empty bottle of water on the flowered oilcloth of the table.

Another friend sent me the only thing he had rescued from the mementos left hanging on the walls after the family had taken away anything of value including his instruments. It was a photograph of Thanassis and me singing with a little boy between us. For some reason we have exchanged hats. He is wearing the sailor's cap Phil gave me, and I'm wearing his broad-brimmed brown fedora. Our eyes are shut and Thanassis' right hand is raised with one finger pointing up as if addressing 'that bastard in the sky.' We're sitting in the combined house and tavern at the back of the village owned by the boy's father, Hasanis. Judging by the hats, we have probably drunk a good deal of Hasanis' home-made wine. There are two hurricane lamps on the shelf above the stone fireplace in case the power is cut off. All through the winter when I was writing the book we had met at Hasanis' to eat, drink and play music. Occasionally the owner would put on a record or strum the bouzouki and Thanassis would rise slowly from his chair to dance a stately *zeibekiko*, his long brown overcoat draped around his shoulders, a Borsalino tipped low over his eyes, his polished shoes winking in the light. His dance was both a parody of the underworld dance of the tough *manghes* of Piraeus, and an expression of what he was: a man who had seen a great deal of the world's ugliness and learned how to keep his distance from it.

For some reason we have exchanged hats

10. War, the Sailor and the Mermaid.

The fact that the man who refused the Italians free passage through Greece had been ruling the country as an illegal dictator, that he had been trained in the Prussian army and was an enthusiastic supporter of Hitler, failed to dampen the Greeks' enthusiasm for the war. With his single "No!" issued to the Italian ambassador, General Metaxas had turned from a fascist-sympathizing tyrant into a national hero over-night. The divisions that had dominated Greek politics since the nation was formed vanished in the intoxication of a small act of defiance that took everyone by surprise, including the man who opened his mouth in the night to say the word that is still marked each year on October 28th by a national holiday: *ohi* day.

What the general did with his 'No' was to unite all Greeks in a de-lirious burst of national pride. Young men and old joined the army to fight the Italians pushing across the border of Albania onto Greek soil. The Greeks were ill-armed and poorly trained, but they were fighting for their homeland; they fought like mad dogs, and they drove the Ital-ians back, village by village, into Albania. By mid-November the radio announced there wasn't an Italian left on Greek soil.

That autumn the first Italian prisoners began arriving in Athens. Their uniforms torn, their faces gaunt and grimy, they gave the Greeks of the capital a feeling of intense satisfaction. To their own surprise the army of this small nation had defeated the enemy. Never mind that the enemy had powerful friends who would certainly be upset by this victory. For the time being there was an atmosphere of carnival in the air. The town buzzed with life, especially at night. The blackouts only encouraged more people to go to the cinema, to the theater, to buy and sell sex on the unlit streets. Those who couldn't enjoy the nightlife knitted. Greek newsreels showed even the sick and the mentally ill knitting for the Greek soldiers on the Front, soldiers who now controlled a quarter of Albania. The first air-raid sirens seemed like sound-effects for the celebrations.

Neither the Greeks nor the Italians were certain of their welcome in the inhospitable mountains that divide Greece from Albania. Some of the Albanians were Muslims who disliked the Greeks and joined the Italians to fight them. Others were Christians or crypto-Christians, and sympathized with the Greeks. Still others were unwillingly conscripted by the Italians. As the fighting dragged on through the winter, snow made the mountain tracks almost impassable; by Spring, mules and horses sank into a sea of mud, drowned in the swollen streams, or slid off the sides of ravines. There was no way to get provisions through to the armies or to carry the wounded out on stretchers. Soldiers on both sides suffered more from frostbite and hunger than from gunshot wounds. The passes were choked with dead animals and men lying where they had fallen in the mud. Two of Greece's greatest modern poets were there, carrying the wounded, and seeing the ugly face of war for the first time. One was Odysseas Elytis, the other, was Nikos Kavadias. Kavadias's account of his war experience was addressed to his horse:

To My Horse
Writing to a person is perhaps easy enough for most people. Writing to an animal is incredibly difficult. That's what I'm afraid of. I won't be able to manage it.

My hands have grown hard from your reins and my soul from other causes. That's why I'm writing to you.

In the beginning you didn't want me. You discerned in me the sloppy, incapable hand. You were right. Maybe it was the first time I'd seen a horse from so close up. All the horses I'd seen in my life were from circuses, trained by

Cossacks, and at the races, where men bet on them. That bothered me. You weren't destined for such low acts. Anyway....that is another story, as Kipling says, he who has loved and written about you so much.

I know how much I tired you. The load set crooked on your back, you followed obediently on the night marches. We quickly became friends. You got used to me. I stopped losing you among the other animals of our unit. I stopped not recognizing you.

If I begin on the "Do you remember?" I'll never finish. I worship brevity. I'll remind you only of three of our nights. (I wonder if I'm myself tonight – I've never spoken so tenderly to anyone before).

Do you remember the night it rained? Unrelenting, and the two of us, soaked to the skin, kept going in the night. Alone. Was I leading you, or you me? I fixed my eyes on the night curtain as I'd never fixed them searching for lights in the North Sea. Your sense of smell saved us. A manger was our refuge. We spread out the hay and lit a big fire. I'm telling you, we lit it. You gave me courage. Lying there I listened to you chewing. Afterwards I spoke to you. I never agreed with people the way I did with you. We fell asleep discussing things. I lying on the hay. You standing. How many people sleep standing up and walking around without half your sense? Anyway...

The second night... the time we went in with a lot of others to the battle. From close in we were able to carry the wounded. Together we heard the noise of war and got used to it. We took the young fellow with the wounded leg and left. I never saw you so careful or walking so lightly. You'd forgotten that nervous habit you had of suddenly jumping and knocking off the saddle. Perhaps you understood it all before I did.

And now, the night on the mountain with the mud: heavily loaded, overtired, we kept going. It's unbelievable the sadness and misery you experience when you feel yourself to be and to see people and animals and everything in the mud.

Fallen horses and mules blocked our road. We went on. Suddenly you fell. We fell, I should say. With your two legs broken, with your head thrust in the mud. Do you remember how I tried? I didn't succeed. You must know very well it wasn't my fault. I never tried so hard. I stayed beside you all night. A little below us a dead Italian soldier. Above us the Great Bear, the Northern Crown, the constellation of Orion scattered a faint light.

I've never seen how people die. I've turned my eyes away from death. But I imagine it...

I'll stop. I'm afraid of saying big words.

I still keep your curry-comb and brush. And when, one day, I give those up, I'll keep you in my memory.

The calluses on my hands from your reins are beloved as those I sometimes get on my sea voyages. I'll write to you again...

Nikos Kavadias, March 1941

Nikos Kavadias

Nikos Kavadias's family was from the small village of Fiskardo on the island of Kefalonia, but Nikos was born in Manchuria in 1913, where his father was a member of a prosperous Greek merchant community. In 1914, fearful of growing violence in the area, Kavadias's father sent his family back to Greece for safety and returned to Manchuria where he disappeared in 1917. Three years later he reappeared like a ghost in Greece, having served three years in a Russian prison. Not only had he lost everything he owned, but he was so shattered by his experience in prison that he would never work again.

Nikos was the eldest child, and had planned to study medicine. From his school days on he wrote his own poems and read French poetry with his sister, Jenia. The loss of his father's fortune forced Nikos to give up his studies and he took a job in the office of one of his maternal uncles, all of whom were in the shipping business. Bored with his office job, Kavadias begged to be allowed to go to sea on one of his uncles' ships as a common sailor. His relatives were shocked at the idea and forbad him to go, but his sister Jenia understood his passion for travel and pleaded his case. At twenty-one he went to sea as a midshipman. A year later he returned with a volume of poems that would have a permanent place in the literary canon of Greece.

The poems of *Marabou* were both old-fashioned and modern; formally they ran counter to the modernist trends of Greek verse, but their subject-matter and language were racy and daring. At a time when his better-known contemporaries had abandoned rhyme and meter, Kavadias insisted on both. When narrative poetry was out of fashion, he told stories of shipboard life. And while his contemporaries struggled to find a language to express the grand themes of neo-Hellenism, or to comment on the political upheavals of the period, Kavadias wrote of black stokers, drunken sea captains, pet monkeys and prostitutes. Kavadias's poems were closer to the lyrics of the rembetika songs than they were to the poetry of his peers, and like the Piraeus song-writers, he looked on the more sordid aspects of life with a merciless eye:

Εἶχε δεξιὰ κι ἀριστερά, ἀπάνω τό ᾽να στ᾽ ἄλλο,
τὰ ξύλινα κρεβάτια μας στὰ πλάγια κολλητά,
ποὺ ἔμοιαζαν, μέσα στὸ θαμπόν, ἀνάλαφρο σκοτάδι,
φέρετρα ποὺ ξεχάστηκαν καὶ μείναν ἀνοιχτά.

One above the other, left and right,
our wooden bunks were attached to the side,
looking, in the gloomy darkness,
like coffins whose lids had been left open.

Σὲ μία γωνιὰ τὸ ἀρμάρι μας, ἀπ᾽ ἔξω στολισμένο
μὲ ζωγραφιὲς χρωματιστὲς ἀπὸ περιοδικὸ
ἢ γαλλικὲς φωτογραφίες αἰσχρές, ποὺ παρασταίνουν
τὸ ἁμάρτημα τῆς ἡδονῆς τὸ προπατορικό.

In one corner our cupboard was adorned
with colored pictures from a magazine
or dirty photos from France that showed
the original sin of Eden: lust.
("Our Fo'cs'le")

Το βράδυ ετούτο κάρφωσε μ᾽ επιμονή το νου μου
κάποια γυναίκα που άλλοτες εγνώρισα, κοινή,
που ωστόσο αυτή ξεχώριζεν από τις αδελφές της,
γιατί ήταν πάντοτε σοβαρή, θλιμμένη και στυγνή.

This evening I recalled some common whore
and wrote a song à la Baudelaire
which, as you read, silent stranger,
will make you laugh at its author with scorn.
("Gabrielle Didot")

It never occurred to me that there would be a problem obtaining the copyright for my translations of Kavadias, especially after a selection of them won a literary prize in New York. I had reckoned without the fierce guardian dragons of literary texts. Jenia Kavadias had been her brother's closest companion, his conspirator in the adventure of becoming a sailor, his literary confidante. She had married, as was expected of her, and been a good wife and mother, but I sensed she had reserved her true passion for her brother and his poetry. When someone asked him to explain a reference in one of his later, more obscure poems, Kavadias would reply, "Ask my sister Jenia." Now it was time for me to ask Jenia for something.

When I met her, Jenia's husband had died and her brother had been dead for a decade. She lived alone near her daughter in an apartment on one of the steepest streets in Athens, a stone's throw from Mariza. Mariza knew that obtaining the rights to Kavadias would not be as easy as I thought: she had battled with Jenia for the rights to set his poems to music. She took me to meet Jenia one evening armed with a large bouquet of flowers. Living with Nikos' poems as I had, poems of a man who had spent his life with common sailors, I was astonished when his sister opened the door. A slim, elegant woman dressed in a navy skirt, a silk blouse and espadrilles, she looked every inch what the Greeks call an *arhontissa*: an aristocrat. On the low tables were the silver boxes and expensive worry-beads that adorn the tables of upper-class Greek apartments. The walls were covered in paintings, drawings, photographs, autographs of Greek poetry, most of them dedicated to her brother, and several framed photographs of him. Jenia was charming, polite, and adamant. No, I could not publish my translations of her brother's poems. They were just too difficult, especially for a foreigner.

"Seferis, yes, Seferis is not so difficult. He doesn't use rhyme, and his poems are influenced by British poetry, particularly by Eliot. Seferis I can imagine. Even Cavafy. He is a poet who has been translated a lot because he is in some ways an international poet; he writes for an international audience. Kavadias loved form, he always used rhyme. If you were to translate the poems using rhyme you couldn't be precise. He was always so precise. There are no wasted words in Kavadias" (I noticed she used the third person when talking about her brother, as if he'd already become a historical figure).

"But how did you get to know his work? What drew you to him?"

I tried to explain why I liked him so much, why his dry, laconic style and his sympathy for his fellow-sailors would appeal to an English-speaking audience.

Jenia looked at me with interest but the conversation had come to an end. She kissed Mariza's plump cheek and held out her hand to me. "I'm sorry," she said. "I'm so glad you like my brother's poems, but I can't give you permission to publish your translations. I don't think you realize how difficult a poet Kavadias is. He may look simple, but for a foreigner to understand Kavadias would take a lifetime."

When we reached the street Mariza looked at my face and smiled.

"Don't give up," she said. "Do you have a spare copy of your book on the rembetika in Greek?"

"Why?" I asked in surprise. "Give it to me. Tomorrow morning I'll have it delivered to Jenia's apartment. When she sees it, she'll change her mind. I have an instinct about these things."

As usual, Mariza was right. While I tried to put the idea of publishing out of my head, her magic was at work. It was only a day before I had a phone call from Jenia.

"If someone had told me that a foreigner could write a book like that about rembetika, I'd never have believed it," she said.

"My brother loved the rembetika. You are the person who will translate Kavadias. But we must work together. When you finish the first book of poems, you can come and stay in my apartment. We'll work on them together."

So began our collaboration and a friendship that lasted until Jenia was nearly blind and had given up the desire to live. She was a demanding collaborator, one that few literary translators would have tolerated. For one thing she laid down rules: I was not to use rhyme because that would risk infidelities to the text. Since her brother was a poet for whom each word mattered ("unlike *some* poets we could name") each word had to be translated. I could play with word order, rhythm, but not too much. Footnotes were to be avoided. Her brother hated explaining his verse. What the reader took away with her or him was all that mattered. As a novice translator I was prepared to obey.

Jenia may have looked like an *arhondissa*, but she was the proud guardian of a body of poems that were largely about sailors and sex. She and I sat in her tiny, cramped apartment, sometimes side by side on the couch, sometimes in the miniscule kitchen, and pondered how we were going to translate "where the girls have it λόξα." Did Kavadias mean they had sex sideways or were their organs supposed to be skewed?" And was the "blond thatch" that covered the Pythian tripod in the poem *Fata Morgana* a reference to pubic hair? Jenia would giggle and forbid me to make anything explicit.

"The publisher understood that the whole poem was about the sexual act," she said, "but he realized that not many of his readers would understand. That's the way it has to be in English too."

What Jenia couldn't help me with was nautical slang. When Kavadias's third volume of poetry was published posthumously, a glossary of nautical terms was supplied for the Greek reader. I doubt if Kavadias would have approved. As Jenia reminded me, he disliked explanations, and she had never troubled herself with precise definitions of ship's slang, but I knew I would have to come up with English equivalents for these terms.

Most Greek sailors' slang can be traced to the Venetians, who dominated Levantine trade for centuries, and some of it is Turkish. Few

Greeks who have not worked aboard Greek ships understand it. Even when I discovered the meaning of a particular word in the glossary at the back of Kavadias's last book or in some dictionary, I still had to find an equivalent in English. Fortunately, I had the resources of an excellent library at my disposal; I found it contained several compendia of British nautical slang, but I was still struggling with the Greek originals. It was only by chance that I discovered, in some catalogue, a book that became a treasured companion on my voyages with Kavadias. It was called *The Lingua Franca in the Levant.* How grateful I was to the scholars and to their esoteric project of compiling a dictionary of the nautical slang of the eastern Mediterranean. Dictionaries become the translator's most treasured possessions, but specialized dictionaries are to the general dictionary as misprinted stamps to their perfect equivalents. They are only of interest to the connoisseur, for whom they become priceless.

Kavadias was the first poet whose work I translated in its entirety. I worked on him not because I had a publisher asking me for a manuscript but because I loved his poems. Soon I began to love the man as well as his poems. I longed to be invited, like his friend, the poet Kaisar Emmanuel, to join him on his voyages:

Τὰ βράδια, βάρδια κάνοντας, θὰ λέγαμε
παράξενες στὴ γέφυρα ἱστορίες,
γιὰ τοὺς ἀστερισμοὺς ἢ γιὰ τὰ κύματα,
γιὰ τοὺς καιρούς, τὶς ἄπνοιες, τὶς πορεῖες.

Ὅταν πυκνὴ ἡ ὁμίχλη θὰ μᾶς σκέπαζε,
τοὺς φάρους θὲ ν᾽ ἀκούγαμε νὰ κλαῖνε
καὶ τὰ καράβια ἀθέατα θὰ τ᾽ ἀκούγαμε,
περνώντας νὰ σφυρίζουν καὶ νὰ πλένε.

Μακριά, πολὺ μακριὰ νὰ ταξιδεύουμε,
κι ὁ ἥλιος πάντα μόνους νὰ μᾶς βρίσκει·
ἐσεῖς τσιγάρα «Κάμελ» νὰ καπνίζετε,
κι ἐγὼ σὲ μία γωνιὰ νὰ πίνω οὐΐσκυ.

Καὶ μία γριὰ στὸ Ἀννάμ, κεντήστρα στίγματος,
- μία γριὰ σ᾽ ἕνα πολύβοο καφενεῖο -
μία αἱμάσσουσα καρδιὰ θὰ μοῦ στιγμάτιζε,
κι ἕνα γυμνό, στὸ στῆθος σας, κρανίο.

At night on the bridge when we were on watch
to pass the time we'd tell tall tales
of constellations and giant waves
of the weather, of calms, and the courses we'd run.

When fog or mist would cover the ship
we'd hear the lighthouse hoot in the grey
and listen to ships we couldn't see
passing and tooting as they sailed on by.

We'd travel far off to unknown lands;
the sun would always find us alone;
you'd be smoking a Camel cigarette
and I'd drink whiskey in a corner nearby.

A little old woman who does tattoos
in a noisy café I know in Annam
would draw for me a bleeding heart
for you, a naked skull on your chest.
  ("Letter to the Poet Kaisar Emmanuel")

Translation is, for me, a luxury, a flight from one's own creative life, and Kavadias was the perfect poet to elope with. I sailed off with him to the New Hebrides and the Bay of Biscay aboard freighters and passenger ships, and we stepped off together to enter a brothel in Marseilles or a bar in Annam. I began my voyage at a difficult time in my life. I had been married for a year and already had two miscarriages. I didn't know, then, that there would be much worse times to come, and how much I would rely on Kavadias to take me on board his rusty freighter.

Jenia understood this. The third summer I visited her she said. "I'm not a metaphysical person, but I know something. You didn't choose to translate my brother; he chose you."

Kavadias seemed to sustain us both in those years. In Ithaca, I would turn from teaching or studying with guilty delight to my translations. On summer trips to Greece I would ring the bell of Jenia's apartment and she would hold me in her thin arms like a lost treasure. In Greek fashion, she would feed me first, but she was always impatient to see what I had done. Sitting with me and working on my translations, Jenia lived, for a few days, with her lost brother. As we progressed to the second and third volumes of his poems, and Kavadias grew older and sadder, she explained to me why he had written the line "and the youngest one sleeps on a Japanese hill." Their younger brother had followed Nikos into the merchant navy and become a captain. Kavadias, who never became a captain but trained as a *marconi* – a radio officer—was proud of his brother. One day, when the young captain's ship was in port at Kobe, he was found dead in his cabin. The cause of his death appeared to be natural, but it remained a tragic mystery to Nikos, something he only referred to in a single line of verse.

Life at sea, despite its exotic pleasures, was also filled with the boredom of long night watches, the endless smutty stories and dirty pin-ups in the fo'cs'le, the fear of cyclones, the whores of the ports and their diseases. After his first book was hailed by the critics as the work of a genuine and original voice in Greek literature, Kavadias might well have settled for a life in Athens, frequenting literary salons and finding some way to earn a living on shore, but he hated literary gatherings and his passion for the sea remained irrational and constant.

Kavadias understood that he had become unfit for life on shore. The disease of the sailor, he wrote, is not sea-sickness but *steriani zali*: shore-sickness. To his friends and fellow-writers in Athens, the sailor poet sent invitations in verse, urging them to abandon the boredom of the city and join him on his adventures:

Το πειρατικό του Captain Jimmy,
που μ' αυτό θα φύγετε και σεις,
είναι φορτωμένο με χασίς
κι έχει τα φανάρια του στην πρύμη.

Μήνες τώρα που `χουμε κινήσει
και με τη βοήθεια του καιρού
όσο που να πάμε στο Περού
το φορτίο θα το έχουμε καπνίσει.

Captain Jimmy's pirate ship
the one that you will leave on too
is carrying a cargo of hashish
and has its lights fixed on the stern.

It's months ago since we set out
and if the weather helps a bit
by the time we've reached Peru
we'll have smoked what's in the hold.
(From "Armida")

The adventures of the sailor don't have happy endings. Drunkenness, disappointed love, and an early death met many of Kavadias' companions. The poem "Southern Cross" begins with a conversation between the protagonist and a member of the crew. The poem ends with a farewell to a love-crossed fellow-sailor:

Σ' ένα μαγαζί του Nossi Be
πήρες το μαχαίρι δυο σελίνια
μέρα μεσημέρι απά στη λίνια
ξάστραψες σαν φάρου αναλαμπή

Κάτω στις ακτές της Αφρικής
πάνε χρόνια τώρα που κοιμάσαι
τα φανάρια πια δεν τα θυμάσαι
και το ωραίο γλυκό της Κυριακής

In some shop in Nosy Bé
you bought the knife – two shillings it cost –
right on the equator, exactly at noon;
it glittered like a lighthouse beam.

Down on the shores of Africa
for some years now you've been asleep.
You don't remember the lighthouse now
or the delicious Sunday sweet.

Kavadias was a romantic. He loved women and he loved the sea. He knew they were incompatible loves, and he chose the sea, but the figure of a woman haunted his dreams, especially on the long night watches. By his third and last volume of poems, *Traverso*, the sea and the woman of his dreams had merged into a single, elusive, dangerous mirage:

Πράσινο. Αφρός, θαλασσινό βαθύ και βυσσινί.
Γυμνή. Μονάχα ένα χρυσό στη μέση σου ζωστήρι.
Τα μάτια σου τα χώριζαν εφτά Ισημερινοί
μες στου Giorgione το αργαστήρι.

Βαμμένη. Να σε φέγγει φως αρρωστημένο.
Διψάς χρυσάφι. Πάρε, ψάξε, μέτρα.
Εδώ κοντά σου, χρόνια ασάλευτος να μένω
ως να μου γίνεις Μοίρα, Θάνατος και Πέτρα.

Green. Foam, navy-blue and purple.
Naked. Just a gold belt at your waist.
Seven parallels divided your eyes
in Giorgione's Venetian studio.

Painted woman. May a sickly light shine on you!
You thirst for gold. Take, search, count.
Here, beside you, I'll stay for years
until you become for me Fate, Death, and Stone.

(From "Woman")

Greek folklore is full of mermaids and Sirens. Kavadias wrote one of his longest and most sensuous poems to *Fata Morgana*, the mirage of a beautiful woman that sailors first saw in the Straits of Messina:

Θὰ μεταλάβω μὲ νερὸ θαλασσινὸ
στάλα τὴ στάλα συναγμένο ἀπ' τὸ κορμί σου
σὲ τάσι ἀρχαῖο, μπακιρένιο ἀλγερινό,
ποὺ κοινωνοῦσαν πειρατὲς πρὶν πολεμήσουν.

Ποῦθ' ἔρχεσαι; Ἀπ' τὴ Βαβυλῶνα.
Ποῦ πᾶς; Στὸ μάτι τοῦ κυκλῶνα.
Ποιὰν ἀγαπᾶς; Κάποια τσιγγάνα.
Πῶς τὴ λένε; Φάτα Μοργκάνα.

I'll take communion with salty water
infused from your body drop by drop
in an ancient goblet of Algerian bronze
that pirates communed with before they fought.

Where are you from? From Babylon.
Where are you going? To the eye of the cyclone.
Whom do you love? A gypsy woman.
What is her name? Fata Morgana.

Mariza Koch sings her setting of Nikos Kavadias's poem "Fata Mogana": goo.gl/0mgAF4

Fata Morgana is probably another name for Morgan le Fey, sister of King Arthur. In Modern Greek folklore, Alexander the Great also has a mermaid sister called *Thessaloniki, Kyna,* or simply *Gorgona* (Greek for a mermaid). On his travels to the Far East, Alexander had, according to the story, found the water of eternal life. When he fell ill with a fever and was near death, he asked for the vial of water he had brought back from his travels and had kept for this moment. Horrified, his sister realized she had accidentally thrown it away. Later, crazed with grief at his death, she threw herself into the waves, but she was so beautiful that the sea took pity on her and transformed her into a mermaid.

From that day on she has been searching for her dead brother through the waters of Greece, asking the captain of each passing ship if he is still alive. The wise captain's reply is: "He lives and reigns and rules the world." The answer satisfies the beautiful mermaid and she sinks beneath the surface; the sea turns glassy, the ship arrives safely in port. If the captain is foolish enough to reply that her brother died years ago, the mermaid lashes her fishy tail and tilts the bowsprit towards the bottom of the sea.

The mermaid can also be, especially on the island of Lesbos, a strange double for the Virgin Mary. Fishing-boats are usually dedicated to Saint Nicholas or to the Virgin, but that doesn't stop them having a mermaid on the prow. In his novel *The Mermaid Madonna*, Stratis Myrivilis, a native of Lesbos, describes a painting of this curious hybrid on the wall of a local taverna;

Her head is painted in the conventional Byzantine style – a dark face, delicately-drawn, its expression reserved, a rounded chin, almond eyes, and a small mouth. A purple veil surrounds her torso and covers her head down to her eyebrows. There is the usual golden halo, as in all icons. Her eyes are extraordinarily wide and green. But from the waist down she is a fish with blue scales; in one hand she holds a ship and in the other a trident like Poseidon's.

The incongruity, some would say blasphemy of the 'Mermaid Madonna' doesn't puzzle sailors and islanders. The mermaid is, after all, a metaphor for virginity, her sexuality terminated at the waist. Kavadias and his fellow sailors were raised on tales of beautiful women who lured sailors to their deaths, but who also offered a kind of salvation. The sea that saves the sailor from a dull life on shore and from the ties of marriage has her own means of enslavement; she is a demanding mistress.

Kavadias would like to have died at sea, but instead he died on shore as he prophesied:

Κι εγώ που τόσο επόθησα μια μέρα να ταφώ
σε κάποια θάλασσα βαθειά στις μακρινές Ινδίες,
θα 'χω ένα θάνατο κοινό και θλιβερό πολύ
και μια κηδεία σαν των πολλών ανθρώπων τις κηδείες.

And I who longed to find my grave
in some sea of the Indies far away
will have a sad and common death,
a funeral like those of other men.
(From, "Mal du depart")

Ten years ago a Turkish friend sent me a CD recorded by a singer who became very popular in Turkey at the turn of the 20th century. Her name was Deniz Kizi Eftalia (the Mermaid Eftalia). She was the daughter of a Greek officer who served in the Ottoman army. On the cover of the CD was the story of how she got her nickname. The twelve-year-old would sing for her father and his drinking-mates, her voice drifting over the Bosphorus so that the people on the shore thought they were hearing a mermaid sing. Despite the poor quality of the recordings, I could hear she had an extraordinary voice. As a Christian, the taboo on a woman making a recording may not have applied to her. In any case, Eftalia is thought to have been the first woman to make a record (in the form of a wax cylinder) in Turkey. I wrote a poem about her.

The Mermaid Eftalya

Summer nights on the Bosphorus
she and her father, a Greek
officer in the Ottoman army
liked to hire a caique
and catch the breeze off the water.
She would sing while he,
fanned by her song, drank raki.

Hearing her voice from banks
they called her "mermaid," a name
she used as she made her debut,
a teenager still. Her fame
increasing year by year
she sang in the Galata cafés
recording her songs for Pathé.

One moonlit night – her birthday —
she sailed the Bosphorus again,
a flotilla of fans in her wake.
All who heard her claimed
the fantastic price worth paying,
her voice was never more
enchanting : "Mermaid, encore!"

they cried and she sang on,
charming them till the moon set.

She shivered in the damp air;
a muezzin called from a minaret
but the mermaid couldn't answer:
her voice was gone. She never
sang again, and died of a fever.

It was Mariza's setting of "Fata Morgana" that had first inspired me to translate Kavadias. It didn't occur to me then that she had something of the mermaid about her. She simply sat on the beach at Faleron and sang me a magical song. In the mid 1990's, when she created a children's show called "The Mermaid Takes Little Alexander for a Ride" it was suddenly clear to me and to the children of Athens that she was a perfect mermaid, that her long blond hair and flowing dresses, her light green eyes, and siren's voice were waiting for this moment of transformation. Tens of thousands of children came to see her as a mermaid; they sent her drawings of mermaids with long blond hair, they brought her mermaid dolls, and mermaid brooches. No wonder they were enchanted; she carried them over the sea to every part of Greece in music familiar to each region and in verses of her own:

The mermaid holds little Alexander in front
and shows him the distant peaks of Rhodope;
the steps of Digenis echo here:
for him Thrace and Asia were a stride apart.

On her way she talks and sings him sweet songs
and over the foam they hug the coast.
She slips into the water and plays with the waves
frightening the ships with her fishy tail

Listen to the song here: goo.gl/0mgAF4

For me "The Mermaid Takes Little Alexander for a Ride" had other connections. The idea for the children's show grew out of a record she had made a year earlier called "The Ways of Little Alexander," a strange, wordless piece of music that she created in memory of my son, Sacha, who was born in 1985. I had brought my son proudly to Greece to meet Mariza and Jenia Kavadias when he was eighteen months old. He died two years later after a long illness. When Mariza heard the news, she remembered the half hour when I had left him with her while I ran to do an errand in Athens. Instead of trying to speak to him, she had made the sounds all Greek mothers make to their babies, holding him on her well-upholstered hip and singing the nonsense syllables that are the foundations of language, the ooh's and ah's of her Greek vowels, the ts's and kh's of her Greek consonants.

For days after I told her of his death, she could think of nothing else but how she had made noises to communicate with a baby she would never see again. Then she began to record sounds older than song itself: weeping, sighing, and laughing sounds, a lullaby that is also a lament. Later she found a musician from an Aegean island who could play almost any Greek instrument. Together they went to a studio and made a recording that was her gift to me.

When I listened to it with her the next summer, she told me how she had explored not only the sounds of the Greek alphabet, but all the modes or, as they are called in Greek music, the "roads", or "ways" of Greek folk music and of Byzantine chant, singing them as if she were teaching a small child. "They're all in there," she said. "All the sounds of Greek music, all the vowels and consonants, everything I know."

"Mariza, it's a music lesson fit for a prince," I said, "Not just for any baby. You could imagine a king searching for the best singer in the land to teach his son like this."

It was somehow a comfort that Mariza had created music for my own lost Alexander. She called the record "The Ways of Little Alexander." Greeks took it to be about the young conqueror of the world. I knew it was about my son, Sacha. I have given the music to the parents of small children ever since, and they all say it has a miraculous effect, soothing a baby's crying as soon as they put it on. I'm not at all surprised. Like almost everything Mariza does, there is something magical about it. She had made a mermaid's song into a memorial, a lullaby, a lesson for a prince, a gift for a grieving mother.

11. After Life

In her book *Death's Door*, Sandra Gilbert muses on the implausibility of death to the living. The unexpected death of her husband leads Gilbert to roam through a wide range of literary sources to see how the writers she and her husband both devoted their lives to dealt with their bereavement in poetry or prose. One of the authors she turns to is Rudyard Kipling, who lost a daughter at age seven and a son in the First World War. A devoted father, he dealt with his grief by imagining his daughter in a romantic afterlife where fountains played and peacocks preened. As Gilbert and Kipling himself was aware, the living cannot move through death's door to the fictive world they invent for their dead. Death's door swings shut with a finality that can only be breached in fantasy, and then only briefly. Gilbert soon turns to another Victorian, Tennyson, whose fantasies of a still-open door between the two worlds soon falter in his great elegy *In Memoriam*. His own wildly unstable mood, induced by the loss of his great friend, has made him "that delirious man/Whose fancy fuses old and new."

Fantasies about the afterlife are common to laments for the dead from most cultures. For the duration of the mourning rituals, death's door swings open like those of a western saloon, offering a brief glimpse of the dark interior. What struck me about the laments of the modern Greek tradition was the ugliness of the vision the mourners glimpse. Far from Kipling's lovely garden, the ghastly, even ghoulish underworld evinced in laments from every corner of Greece make no distinction between Paradise, Hades, or Tartarus. Whatever its name, the after-world is a place where the body decays and is eaten by worms, snakes or Death himself. The singer of laments is the only living person who can penetrate this world, and she acts as a go-between for the community. Unlike the Christian Hell, the Greek underworld is not a place of punishment. The dead are tormented not because of any sin they may have committed on earth, but because *Charos* (Death), imagined occasionally as a boatman like his classical ancestor *Charon*, but more commonly as a horseman riding a black horse, has carried them off to a place that no-one in his right mind would wish to inhabit.

The recent dead speak through the intermediary of the lament singer as if to crush any pleasant fantasy the living may have about the afterlife. The lament-singer briefly opens the door, only to slam it shut without a word of consolation:

Άνοιξε χείλι κρίνε μου και στόμα μίλησέ μου
και γλώσσα μου παραγλυκειά γλυκά κουβεντιασέ μου
και πες μου πως επέργασες αυτού στον κάτω κόσμο.
Κ'εκείνος αποκρίθηκε με χείλι πικραμένο,
«Μη δα βρα νιούς και γέροντες και νιές να καμαρώνουν
μη δα την πρωτομαγιά ψιλά να τραγουδίσω.
Εδώ ηύρα νιούς ξαρμάρτατους και νιές ξεστολισμένες
εδώ ηύρα και νοικοκύρες σα θύρες γκρεμισμένες
εδώ ηύρα πλούσιους και άρχοντες σα δέντρα κουφωμένα
εδώ ηύρα και βαρυάρρωστους σα μήλα μαραμένα
ηύρα μικά τράνα παιδιά να κλαίνε και τη μάνα.

Open your lips, my lily, and mouth, speak to me
and sweetest tongue, sweetly converse with me
and tell me how you've spent your time in the underworld.
And he answered with bitter lips:
"I didn't find young men or old or girls in their pride.
I didn't find the first day of May to raise my voice in song.

Here I found young men disarmed and girls stripped of their finery.
Here I found good housewives like ruined towers,
Here I found rich men and nobles like hollow trees.
Here I found the deathly ill like rotten apples,
I found flocks of little children crying for their mothers."

But does she shut the door? It is the dead, in her lament, who address the living with words that can only increase the sorrow of the bereaved. The pattern is common to thousands of laments: the lamenter questions the dead about the underworld. The dead responds with a morbid vision of what awaits the living after death. Why?

Laments act as a bridge between two worlds, and are thought of as speaking the truth about the dead. In ancient Greece the worst thing that could befall a man was to die "unwept and unburied". The two activities, burial and lament, are not only intertwined; they are singled out as the essential rituals of mourning. A handful of dust, thrown by Antigone on the body of her brother, and her own cries of grief are sufficient to fulfill the duties of a relative to the dead. In cultures like Greece, where the dead are disinterred and reburied, the entire community has a chance to witness what the earth does to the body. What laments refer to in what we would consider ghoulish detail — the decomposition of the body— is, on one level, desirable. The worms and snakes of Death that devour the body perform a function, "dissolving" the flesh so that the bones can be reburied in an ossuary. It is a fortunate sign for the relatives when the bones of the dead are clean. If the flesh has not parted from the bones, it is taken as an ominous sign. Clean bones are carefully washed with wine to make sure no flesh adheres before they are placed in an urn. Laments are sung again for the reburial. The belief that the bones of the dead should be clean is remarkably widespread and seems to be associated with beliefs about the pollution of flesh.

In Greece, where the bodies of dead husbands, mothers, wives, and children are dug up and the bereaved are responsible for washing and handling the bones, the harsh rhetoric of laments becomes comprehensible. Could anyone who has participated in such a ceremony cling to a fantasy like Kipling's of a rosy afterlife? Strangely, the same Greek women who sing laments for the dead describe themselves as Orthodox Christians. They participate in the Easter ceremony and greet one another with the customary Easter Day exchange: "Christ is risen!" "Truly arisen!"

How do they square the two conflicting sets of beliefs, the pagan rhetoric of the laments and those the Church teaches? Only, we can speculate, by disembodying Christ and the saints. The bodies of Saints are described by believers as having no smell, or a pleasant smell. While they offer prayers for the dead and ask the Virgin Mary to intercede for them, the villagers also believe in the relationship between pain and truth, and the pain of grief legitimates the lament-singer's words.

If laments tell the pain-filled truth, they also insist on the beauty of the natural world. The underworld is a perfect mirror image of the sun-lit upper world, which is evoked in all its beauty by the envious dead. Above all the dead long for light:

Ο κάτω κόσμος ειν' κακός γιατί δε ξημερώνει
Γιατί δεν κράζει ο πετεινός δεν κελαδεί τ'αηδόνι

The underworld is bad because day never breaks
because the cock doesn't crow and the nightingale never sings.
(From Rhodes, Saunier: 324)

Στον κάτω κόσμο δε φωτάει κι ήλιος ποτές δε βγαίναι,
ούτε νερό δε βρίσκεται, σαπούνι δεν πουλιέται,
Για να νιφτούν οι άνιφτοι, να πιούν οι διψασμένοι.

In the underworld the sun doesn't shine, it never comes out.

nor is their water, they don't sell soap
for the unwashed to clean themselves, for the thirsty to drink.
(From Koroni – Methoni. Saunier:324)

Through the medium of the lament, the dead seem to be warning the living to hold on to what they have: the beauty of the world above. Curiosity about the other world is natural but bound to lead to unwanted truth. A lament found all over Greece with minor variation describes the visit of a bird from the underworld:

Ένα πουλάκ εξέβγαινεν από τον κάτω κόσμο.
Είχε τα νύχια κόκκινα και τα φτερά του μαύρα,
τα νύχι' από τα αίματα και τα φτερ' απ' το χώμα.
Τρέχουν μανάδες για να διούν κ'οι αδερφές να μάθουν,
γυναίκες των καλών ανδρών να πάρουν την αλήθεια.
Η Μάνα φέρει ζάχαρι κ' η αδερφή το μόσχο,
γυναίκες των καλών ανδρών αμάραντο στα χέρια.
—φάγε πουλί το ζάχαρι κι από το μόσχο,
μυρίσου τον αμάραντο, για να μας μολογήεις.
—Καημένες, τ'ειδα, τι να πω και τι να μολογήσω;
Ειδα τον Χαρο κ'έτρεχε στους κάμπους καβαλλάρης,
σέρνει τους νιούς απ' τα μαλλιά, τους γέρους απ' τα χέρια,
φέρνει και τα μικρά παιδιά στη σέλλ'αρμαθιασμένα.

A little bird came from the underworld;
its claws were red, and its feathers black,
the claws from blood, feathers from earth.
Mothers run to see it, brothers to discover,
wives of good men to learn the truth.
The mother brings sugar and the sister muscatel,
wives of good men bring amaranth in their hands.

"Eat the sugar, bird and drink the muscatel,
smell the amaranth so you can tell us all."
"Poor things, I saw them, what can I say, what can I reveal?
I saw Death racing through the field on horseback;
he drags young men by the hair, old men by the hands,
he brings little children threaded on his saddle.
(Saunier 380)

The macabre bird from the underworld is, like the lament-singer herself, simply a messenger. Despite its sinister appearance, it seems as saddened by the sights of the underworld as the bereaved, and reluctant to reveal the truth about the horrors of the afterlife. *"Ti na mologiso?"* the bird asks (literally, what can I confess?) as if the truth is too painful for the bereaved to bear.

Rather than console or dampen the grief, laments exaggerate or heighten its intensity. From bodily gesture to sobs and cries, to words that offer not relief but black despair, the lament-singer ratchets the mood of sorrow to a climax that is close to madness. For the duration of their lament they venture into the world behind the swinging door of death, a door that must not be opened by the living. Specialized in grief and its rituals, they assume the weight of loss for a time, entering into a perilous dialogue with the dead, but they will return empty-handed, encouraging the bereaved to feel the full horror of their grief. Burning themselves with tears, stabbing themselves with harsh words, the community will indulge in grief to the full. Neither comfort nor consolation is offered.

Laments are in formal meter. Meter is both an aid to spontaneous composition, in that it has a built-in repertoire of formulaic structures that can be adapted to a particular occasion, and a stimulus to memory. Echoing phrases and repetition also act as aids to memory. In this powerful lament from Epirus in Northern Greece, the common device of parallel phrasing is extended to a metaphor of a desired but impossible exchange.

Χάρε τον νιόν οπού κτρατεις, Χάρε τον νέον οπό' χεις,
Κάμε και χάρισέ τον μας και πίσο στείλε το μας
Και παρ'οκάδες μάλαμα κι' οκά μαργαριτάρι
Και κάμε και τη θάλασσα κάμπο και περιβόλι
Και κάμε και τ'αγρια βουνά λιμένα και ακρογιάλι.
Μήγαρις βέργα χάσαμε μήγαρις δακτυλίδι
Χάσαμ' οκάδες μάλαμα οκάδες τσοβαϊρι.

Death, the youth you are holding, Death, the youth you have,
do this — give him to us, and send him back to us
and take pounds of gold and pounds of pearls
and make the sea field and garden
and make the wild mountains harbors and shore.
We lost a birch rod, we lost a ring.
We lost pounds of gold, pounds of precious stones.
(Saunier:1999:204)

The melodic structure of laments is also formal, even if pitch and rhythm may be interrupted or "bent" by the emotional intensity of the performance. The melodic shape, if not the entire tune of a lament is familiar to the singer and the listener. Independently of the text, it signals death and bereavement. Indeed, wordless laments are common to many cultures, including Scotland and Greece. Certain melodic modes come to be associated with loss and death, and their sound has the ability to evoke strong emotions in the listener. It is the recognition of the familiar, the shared knowledge of a tradition that makes laments so effective as a stimulus to collective memory. The lament-singer who draws on a repertoire of appropriate verse and melody, tone and rhythm to improvise a lament has already evoked, in her audience, the memory of numerous other deaths; her work is to go beyond this general mood of mourning and create a dialogue with the individual dead. This dialogue, if it is judged effective, is then folded back into the communal memory to be re-used with minor alterations on another occasion.

It is impossible to disentangle the performance of lament from communal memory. Laments are performed for an "audience" of relatives and fellow-villagers in the context of the rituals of mourning. They are addressed both to the dead and to the members of the community. How "well" they are performed is judged on the basis of assumptions about a desirable relationship between affect and control. They do not so much "remember" the dead as summon him or her to the presence of the living. As lament singers have told me, they use the pain of their own personal loss to create the effect they need to "perform grief" at the funeral of another. The mourners gathered at the village funeral may share feelings of grief, but each individual mourner may focus on the memory of her lost child or husband. The dead body at the center of the funeral is a trigger for private memory at the very moment when her/his life is being inscribed into the communal memory in the form of a lament.

Before I left Greece in 1980 I had become interested in the folk laments for the dead. When my son died I began reading the texts of these laments, not as comfort but because they were songs for the inconsolable. Strangely, it was a sort of bleak comfort to recognize that women had lived through this experience before, some of them not once but two or three times.

I began to write about laments as an academic. That gave me a certain amount of control over the material. At a Greek funeral, the immediately bereaved usually don't sing laments. Others do it for them. The bereaved wait, and if they have the skill, they make a lament at the funeral of another. It took me decades to write my own laments...

Well-water

When his mother died
in the village in Epirus
the clarinet-player went back
to sit by the body
through the long night
of laments. She was old
and he shed no tears
while the women sang.

When morning came
he went out for a cigarette
and cried like a baby.
That's what laments do,
he told me — the deeper you dig
the more you find,
like water in a well.

Old Grief

Old grief is like groundwater,
invisible unless
you dig deep, or like
a ground bass that
anchors a baroque concerto,
necessary and unnoticed.

Above ground are the tunes
we hear, notes played
by soloists on treble instruments.
Beneath, the bass descends
in step-wise motion
down to where a shiver

in the chest defines its pitch.
Only the deaf can hear it
and bass-players who hold
their big fiddles close
to their chests, feeling the shudder
of each note that rises from the depths.

Grit

It took twenty years
to coat the grit of grief.
At first it chafed and gouged
beyond bearing but
I blunted its raw edges
with nacreous juice until
I swaddled it smooth.

It hangs dead center
of my throat flanked
by lesser orbs, each
numbed to a roundness
by the work of mourning.
Only yours is perfect:
it took the cunning of a mother
to make this pearl.

Memorials

The best are not by design:
a dome left whole at Hiroshima,
a stopped clock at Skopje,
the high-water mark in New Orleans.
These are what wrench the heart.

Monuments meant to mourn
for all tend instead
to distract the mind's eye.
They planted a garden for my son;
the scar on my belly still aches.

Ami

for Chana Kronfeld

The perfect sphere that rested
on the gray matter beneath
the skull grew no bigger
than a pea before you
lost the English word
for anger and retrieved the Hebrew.

Most would be satisfied with that
but you tossed and turned
until a scan revealed
the poisonous intruder
in what the doctor called
"your beautiful brain."

At the Funeral

At your funeral I remembered his.
One death doesn't make
the next easier; their weight combines
like shovels of dirt on a pine box.

At his funeral I had no words.
I stood at the center of things dumb
and blinded, grief clouding me
like the ink of a giant squid.

Ami, forgive me. At your funeral
I thought of my son in your mother's house,
the day we washed him in the kitchen sink
and how he laughed. Even grief is selfish.

My grief for you got mixed up
with grief for him. At one funeral
we remember another. It's how we know
nothing is lost. Pain has perfect recall.

Hope

Hope is the tease in the short skirt
caroling a tune in a major key
as she turns the corner; a shameless flirt,
she doesn't believe in delivery.

Hope's music is never ended;
outside my window late at night
I can still hear her song in my head
with its talk of roses and candlelight.

Now I know it's a fantasy —
I've tried too often to sing along —
I thought she'd stop from courtesy
but she keeps singing her silly song.

Evergreen

The forest gives me the green light
to talk to my dead. In its glow
I tell you how I miss you,
how ageless you are in memory.

The tender leaves of late spring
clench their green fists like a baby's,
not ready to splay their fingers;
I can still feel yours in mine.

And how like my mother's mine are,
blue veins ramifying from wrist
to ring-finger. I found that lost sapphire,
remember, when I was only six?

"Fireworks" you called me, Dad.
Was I so volatile or just
a chip off your cockney block,
my walk as light, my life not so lucky?

My loves, I talk to you in the woods
that shelter us from the noisy world.
Only here, in its green, can I sense you
ageless and speechless, listening to me.

Bees

Inexperienced at funerals the daughters added
sugar to the dish of boiled wheat
they laid on her grave and bees came
by the thousand, unsettling priests and a bishop.
The daughters weren't afraid. The next year

when they dug up their mother's bones
for reburial, they washed them
in sweet wine instead of dry
and bees came again - a brown cloud
buzzing through the open window.

The daughters thought the skull
would be hardest, but the ribs were worse,
a cage that once rose with her breath.
They should have put the bones straight
in an urn but they were alive with bees.

Should a Man Teach his Son to Plough?

for David Grossman

Into what reality are our children raised?
you asked. Should a man who lives
on a battlefield teach his son to plough?

Without you he'll learn
to load a rifle, fit its butt
to the shoulder's hollow, where

a woman lays her head after love.
Should a man teach his son to plough
so he'll understand the field of Mars

is fertilized with blood and bone?
What's he to plant in a paddock of war?
Forget-me-nots? Landmines?

He learns to plant olives here,
burn them there, speak a language
prized from prayers and dead scrolls

to make poems with, make love
before he fastens his flak-jacket
and takes the ploughed field.

Wells

Why the clump of bare trees
on a hillside satisfies the eye
more than a single tree,
or a clutter of birds on the feeder,
a swath of spring bulbs,
a heap of oranges beside the road
near Argos, children in the schoolyard
gathered in what Greeks call
little wells, wells
of talk, teasing, gossip,
wells of women laughing
old men drinking,
musicians passing phrases,
cows sharing the shade
of an oak, wary cats
in the village square,
tombstones clumped by clan
on the cemetery lawn,
little wells of the dead.

12. Mauthausen

The words of the song rise above the square. Few of the thousands standing shoulder to shoulder in the soft May sunshine can understand them but after an hour of speeches, mostly in German, they are happy to hear another language, to hear music that is familiar to many of them, independent of its Greek words:

Τι ωραία που είν' η αγάπη μου
με το καθημερνό της φόρεμα
κι ένα χτενάκι στα μαλλιά.
Κανείς δεν ήξερε πως είναι τόσο ωραία.

How lovely is my love
in her everyday dress
with a little comb in her hair.
No-one knew how lovely she was.

Κοπέλες του Άουσβιτς,
του Ντάχαου κοπέλες,
μην είδατε την αγάπη μου;

Girls of Auschwitz
girls of Dachau
have you seen the one I love?

Την είδαμε σε μακρινό ταξίδι,
δεν είχε πια το φόρεμά της
ούτε χτενάκι στα μαλλιά.

We saw her on the long journey.
She didn't have her dress any more
nor the little comb in her hair.

Τι ωραία που είν' η αγάπη μου,
η χαϊδεμένη από τη μάνα της
και τ' αδελφού της τα φιλιά.
Κανείς δεν ήξερε πως είναι τόσο ωραία.

How lovely is my love
The one caressed by her mother
and her brother's kisses.
No-one knew how lovely she was.

Κοπέλες του Μαουτχάουζεν,
κοπέλες του Μπέλσεν,
μην είδατε την αγάπη μου;

Girls of Mauthausen,
girls of Belsen,
have you seen my love?

Την είδαμε στην παγερή πλατεία
μ' ένα αριθμό στο άσπρο της το χέρι,
με κίτρινο άστρο στην καρδιά.

We saw her in the frozen square

with a number on her white arm
and a yellow star over her heart.

Τι ωραία που είν' η αγάπη μου,
η χαϊδεμένη από τη μάνα της
και τ' αδελφού της τα φιλιά.
Κανείς δεν ήξερε πως είναι τόσο ωραία.

How lovely is my love .
The one caressed by her mother
and her brother's kisses.
No-one knew how lovely she was.

To hear the song, visit goo.gl/zu1TWl

We are standing at the center of the former concentration camp of Mauthausen exactly fifty years after it was liberated by a unit of General Patton's Third Army. A retired colonel named Richard Seibel has just described how, on May fifth 1945, he received a radio message: "We've come on something that should be investigated."

It was a little before noon when they reached the camp and a tank broke down the gate. What they saw inside was a vision of hell. To the amazement of the American soldiers, among the human skeletons that struggled to reach the tank and kiss its charred metal, flags began to appear. Scraps of material that had been stolen and sewn, hidden under mattresses in preparation for this day, were pulled out from their hiding places and waved in the air – Czech, Polish, British, and Greek flags. On the day before the liberation, 68, 798 prisoners were counted by the Germans. 658 of them were Greeks, 169 of them Greek Jews.

Iakovos Kambanellis

As I stand listening to the music, I can feel the savage joy of the day of liberation. I have lived in this camp in my imagination for a year, translating the memoir of a man who went on to become Greece's leading playwright, Iakovos Kambanellis. Arrested while trying to escape from occupied Greece with a fellow student, Kambanellis entered Mauthausen in 1943 and left it September 1945 with a secret transport of Jews who were trying to reach Palestine. Twenty years later he published his memoir.

They were wise to stay up there on top of their tanks," he wrote." *They had saved themselves from so many battles. They'd never had saved themselves from our joy. We howled, shook ourselves as if we were demented. We pushed and trod on each other so as to get close to the tank.*

As some prisoners fought their way to the tank, others were taking their revenge. Two Spanish prisoners began skinning a *kapo* alive. Another kapo was being strangled with a belt. The prisoners surged towards the smashed gate of the camp. Two more tanks stood outside, their crews staring in awe at the crazed and starving crowd. Then they saw a still stranger sight. The women of Mauthausen were walking down the road dressed in sacks and rags, their faces hairy with malnutrition, their hair shorn. They broke into the buildings, grabbing curtains, cloths, towels – anything they could transform into some sort of clothing.

I look around me at the crowd, many of whom are young people. There are some older people too, men and women of various nationalities listening to the voice of Maria Farandouri singing the music of Theodorakis. Apart from the speeches, it is the only "event" on the program. When it ends there are tears in many eyes and a spontaneous cheering fills the air. The language of this Greek love song has released the emotion that the long official speeches failed to ignite. How strange it is to hear the music I know so well in this place of death! Stranger still that this song should be based on the *Song of Songs* .

"Sundays," Kambanellis wrote, "were days of love at Mauthausen."

On Sunday afternoons, work stopped in the camp and men and women prisoners, separated by an electrified fence and more than a hundred meters of ground, stared tirelessly at each other. Despite their shaved heads and emaciated bodies, despite malnutrition so severe that all the women had stopped menstruating, their mutual gaze was one of desire.

You felt a jarring in the legs, as if someone buried deep in the earth was beating an enormous drum. If the fences were suddenly to go, men and women would have charged forward in a frenzied mutual rape. The half-dead, bony bodies would have been in pain, screaming, dying.

One Sunday Kambanellis heard a Jewish prisoner beside him reciting...

Behold, thou are fair
my love....

The memory stayed with him, and one day he wrote his own "Song of Songs" for Theodorakis to set to music.

Kambanellis was lucky. He met a German draftsman, a philhellene who managed to get him transferred from the quarry to his office as an assistant and saved him from certain death. But there was another Greek prisoner, a fruit-seller named Andonis, who became a legend in the camp because of what he did here one day. He came to Mauthausen later than Kambanellis, in April 1944, and was immediately placed in solitary confinement. It took the other Greek prisoners a few days to discover that there was another Greek in the punishment section of the camp. From the beginning, it was clear that he had style. When the Greeks approached the barbed wire that isolated him, he began singing. He was able to tell them who he was and how he got to Mauthausen by adjusting his tale to the tune of a popular song called "Maritsa, I'll be at Kastella." He had spent sixteen months in Dachau and had learned to ask for cigarette butts using this song.

Andonis was put to work in the quarry. The survival rate among the prisoners who quarried stone and carried the massive blocks up the one hundred and eighty-six steps to the top was between three weeks and two months. An expendable, constantly renewed labor force, most of the workers were Jews or Russian prisoners of war. On a day that was to become legendary soon after Andonis began working in the quarry, a Jewish prisoner stumbled on the staircase and Andonis helped him to lift his stone. A guard saw the incident and ordered the Jew to run the rest of the way up. He managed only a few stairs before he fell. The guard shot him before he could stand up. Andonis looked straight at the guard and lifted the stone of the dead man in addition to his own. When he came down to pick up his next stone, the guard searched for the largest block he could find.

"That's yours," he said.

Andonis eyed the blocks until he found an even larger one.

"This one is mine," he said.

For the rest of the day Andonis continued to lift and carry the heaviest stones he could find. His behavior thrilled the camp for months. Kambanellis wrote a chapter of his memoir about Andonis, and turned his story into a poem, a song Maria Farandouri is singing in the square:

Ο Εβραίος πέφτει στο σκαλί
και κοκκινίζει η σκάλα
κι εσύ λεβέντη μου έλα εδώ
βράχο διπλό κουβάλα.

The Jew falls on the step
and the stairs turn red,
'And you, my fine fellow, come here,
carry a stone twice as big!'

Παίρνω διπλό, παίρνω τριπλό
μένα με λένε Αντώνη

κι αν είσαι άντρας, έλα εδώ
στο μαρμαρένιο αλώνι.

'I'll take double, triple:
they call me Andonis
and if you're a man, come here
to the marble threshing-floor.'

Listen to the song: goo.gl/e5b3yL

In Greek folk songs, a hero often challenges Death to a wrestling match on one of the circular marble threshing-floors that spot the Greek hillsides like dark coins. Death inevitably wins, usually by foul means, but the hero's pride demands he fight as well as he can. He may even buy himself some extra time if he fights well enough. Somehow Andonis had cheated Death for a year but when they were repatriated he didn't leave with the Greeks to go back to his country. In the camp he had become a legend. In Greece he sold fruit from a barrow in the street. He had dreams of a better life. Perhaps he found a better life. Perhaps he went back, one day, to Greece. No-one ever found out. I hope he heard this song, somewhere, and knew that his moment of defiance had been immortalized.

"When you translate my book," Kambanellis had told me, "see if you can emphasize the beauty of the countryside around the camp. It made it seem more cruel, more unnatural, somehow."

As the music ends and we move off towards the bus at the bottom of the stone quarry, we pass the monuments to the dead set in trim green grass. Birds are singing, and the spring sun shines softly on the stone steps.

Kambanellis' memoir is not only about the horrors of the camp. It is also a love story. Kambanellis fell in love with a Lithuanian Jewish girl shortly after the Americans entered the camp. In the weeks and months that followed, while the American army and the International Red Cross tried to arrange for the repatriation of the prisoners, the two young lovers tried to find happiness, but they were haunted by memories so horrible that they despaired of ever being able to erase them from their memory. Finally they agreed to "exorcise" the past by visiting the sites of the worst atrocities they had witnessed one by one. Already, some of these places had been transformed by the prisoners. Each afternoon, the stairway to the stone quarry, for example, became a place of mourning;

On one step someone had placed flowers and a piece of paper with strawberries on it. On another a name had been written in black paint. Near the middle of the stairway a man was busily rubbing the stair with his hand as if he wanted to get a good hold on it...Further down, a man and a woman were kneeling and prostrating themselves, resting their foreheads on the step above.

The lovers not only revisited the sites of murder and torture, they went on excursions to the surrounding countryside to eat at cafés. Wherever they went the villagers looked at them with resentment. On one such trip they were approached by the widow of one of the most notorious Nazi officers who asked them to intercede on behalf of her husband. Later, when streams of starving refugees from the eastern part of Germany arrived in the area looking for shelter or food, they were greeted with the same hostility as the ex-prisoners. No-one offered them anything, and not even the local police intervened to help them. This infuriated one of the Greek ex-prisoners so much that he went to a farm to take milk from the farmer, and threatened to come back and wreck his house unless he offered shelter to several families. He was afraid that if he left, the farmer would turn the refugees out into the street so he stayed with them, making sure the strangers had a night's rest before they set out again searching for a place to stay.

I walked out of the hotel to the end of the village. It was a warm evening with a strong smell of flowers and cut grass. A signpost pointed to the villages of Pregarten and Schwertberg. I remembered how the people from these towns had joined enthusiastically in the manhunt for the escaped Russian prisoners. The countryside looked as quaintly pastoral as a Dresden shepherdess. Kambanellis was right: the horror of the camp must have seemed even crueler in this beauty.

We were an odd crew. Theodorakis had written asking me if I wanted to join a group of his friends and musicians for a small tour. We would attend the premiere of his opera *Elektra* in Luxemburg. Then we would travel by bus together to Meiningen. There, we would see a concert performance of his first opera, *Medea,* which had had its premiere in Bilbao two years earlier. From Meiningen we would set out for Mauthausen, and finally there would be a concert in Stuttgart to celebrate the composer's 75th birthday.

Besides the musicians, Theodorakis had gathered a group of his oldest friends together. Some he'd known since his student days. Others he had met in Greece's own versions of the concentration camps, the prison islands where the left-wing Greeks were interned during and after the Civil War. As we drove through the green German countryside patched with squares of yellow, they did what Greeks always do when they get together, they argued about politics. One of Theodorakis's oldest friends was an architect from Thessaloniki named Argyris. He had fought on the side of the Left during the war, and was arguing with Theodorakis's cardiologist who had fought on the opposite side.

"At least we had our ideals!" Argyris snorted.

"It all depends on what happens to you, which side you join," said Kostas P., who came from the village of Vizitsi in the Peloponnese.

"Listen," he said, turning to me, "Argyris will tell you everything from the side of E.A.M. (the Communist-led Greek Liberation Front) and I'll tell you the same thing from the other side. Like what happened to my brother. It was when Aris Velouhiotis came down to the Peloponnese. The Peloponnese was regarded as not active enough in the Resistance, and so the "Black Caps" came to the villages and rounded people up. My father and some of the other village leaders were taken to the prison camp that had been set up at a town called Spatha. They were all accused of being traitors. But what could they betray? None of them was political. E.A.M. had forbidden anyone to move without a permit. You couldn't even go to fetch water from the well without a permit. My brother had gone to the next village to bring back some wheat and other supplies we needed. When he got back he headed straight for the camp to see his father. He was only twenty-four, and they killed him as an example to the village not to disobey their orders."

Theodorakis, who was following the bus in a minivan with his wife, had gathered, from the dramatic hand gestures accompanying the argument, that things were getting exciting in the bus, and he signaled the driver to pull over so that he could join in. He climbed on board and was greeted briefly before the squabbling resumed.

"Remember how we fought when we were students?" he said to Kostas, now his heart specialist. "Not just words, but fists and bloody noses."

They both laughed as if it had all been some schoolboy game. The Greeks who lived through the War and Civil War keep returning to the events of those days that had marked them forever. I had listened to such tales many times, but never heard men who fought on opposite sides arguing so amiably about it. What was striking about the accounts of what happened in this or that part of Greece is that everyone seemed to know the individuals involved.

"That must have been Mahairas. His son's the one who's a lawyer."

"Yes, that's the one. They were cousins of Notis, who joined E.A.M. in…"

"And when Aris came they began the executions. He had written off the Peloponnesians as a lot of collaborators. They shot Yiannis Melanos."

"The father of Petros?"

It seemed as if everyone in Greece was related to someone they knew.

Theodorakis had told some of his own war stories and everyone was arguing loudly and laughing when we stopped for lunch at a roadside restaurant. I found myself seated next to a slim, deeply tanned man wearing an elegant hounds-tooth jacket who had been driving behind us in his car.

We introduced ourselves and he told me he used to be Theodorakis's tailor. It was he who made the loose black suits with mandarin collars that became the composer's trademark on his tours. Now he owned a hotel in Crete. His profession, he said, probably saved him from death in the camp.

I looked at him in amazement.

"You were in Mauthausen?"

"Not in the main camp; in one of the annexes, at Melk. We didn't have a crematorium there. Right at the end of the war a gas chamber was built but they never used it."

"Why were you sent there?" I asked him.

"I was a partisan in the Resistance. They arrested me in Hania in 1942. Eight hundred of us Resistance-fighters were sent to the camps, and only one hundred and eighty survived. Kambanellis and myself were lucky — we had special skills. Iakovos had been to art school so they put him in the drafting office. I worked as a tailor, making uniforms for the Nazis. That's why we survived."

A tall young man joined us. Yorgos introduced me to his son and the young man sat beside his father listening politely to a story he must have heard a thousand times.

"We Greeks tended to make friends with the Spanish prisoners. We felt we had something in common, and all we did was try to survive. The Russians were different. They were very defiant and kept trying to escape, so more of them got killed.

"In the beginning, when we were being moved by train from one camp to another, I remember a group of Russian prisoners who all sat on one side of the carriage where the bars were and they started singing. The guards liked the music and they let them go on, but the prisoners at the back of the group were busy sawing through the bars – using the music to cover the noise. When they finished, they jumped off the train, maybe twenty or thirty of them. You should have seen the beating we got because of it!"

Yorgos' schnitzel sits untouched on his plate and I apologize for asking him questions.

He waves his hand in a gesture of deprecation.

"I feel as if it is my duty to talk about these things. And I'll tell you something else. The saddest moment for us was when we got back to Greece. The Greek government didn't want anything to do with us because we had been members of E.A.M.. First they didn't want to help us come back, and then, when we arrived, we were greeted by soldiers waving rifles at us. We thought we were headed straight back to prison, but a woman — actually she was a right-wing member of parliament — said it was a shame to be treating us as if we were criminals when we had fought against the Germans and suffered so much in the camps.

"So they let us go, but I'll never forget that homecoming, and how betrayed we all felt."

Unlike the rest of the group, Yorgos didn't seem to be amused by the jokes about the war. He took Theodorakis and his wife to the car and they waited for the bus to leave. Most of the group was sleepy after lunch, but Argyris, who knew I had written about the rembetika and would find such things interesting, began to give me a long lecture about the *diako-niarides*, a secretive guild of beggars who used to roam the villagers of northern Greece, panhandling. According to Argyris they pooled their resources, trading and selling what they had acquired at a profit. They developed their own slang, a patois no-one outside the clan understood. The most famous of them even had songs written about them. He began to sing one but was interrupted by a Cypriot journalist who had joined us and wanted to talk about Cyprus.

The arguments started again, this time about the Cyprus situation, always a good subject to start a fight over. When they tired of that, the passengers started to argue about the bright yellow fields outside the bus window and what sort of crop might be planted in them.

"Mustard," said one voice.

"Too bright for mustard. It's that stuff they make oil from. Rape seed."

"It's the same as we grow in the North of Greece.

"No, it's different. The yellow is darker."

Nothing will do, in the end, but to ask the driver to pull over. I had to smile as three aging Greeks who had just visited a Concentration Camp, and been arguing over executions in the Civil War and the tragedy of the Turkish invasion of Cyprus, stepped into a field to pick yellow flowers. It is what makes Greeks Greek, this endless wrangling over things large and small, the love of a good argument that makes it worth stopping a bus to settle.

13. Great Expectations — the Burden of Philhellenism

Off Skyros

for Alicia and John

Early in the morning I walk to the sea,
its surface slick as oil on a plate
and break the stillness carefully like separating
an egg. Swimming towards the sun, I contemplate

how many summer mornings are left
sublime as this. Was Brooke aware,
dying off this island, that his grave
would satisfy his prescient prayer,

dug in a field "fragrant with sage
and thyme" as his friend Browne wrote?
No foreign corner this but cornerstone
of all he'd learned in classrooms now remote.

Byron first visited Greece in 1809 and 1810, after which he published the first two cantos of *Childe Harold's Pilgrimage*. Between 1812 and 1821, when the Greek War of Independence began, a dozen editions of the poem had been printed, and it had been translated into the major European languages. Byron, whose name was to become synonymous with Romantic philhellenism, was one of a number of wealthy and adventurous European travelers who made the difficult journey to Greece to view the ruins of antiquity, often collecting as many relics as they could carry back with them. They wrote of the contemporary inhabitants of Greece as if they were the indubitable, if humble descendants of Plato and Aristotle, and aspired to be as free and glorious as their ancestors. If the discrepancy between what they saw and what they expected caused some travelers to wonder whether the present inhabitants might not be in any way related to the ancient Hellenes, they explained the degeneracy as having been caused by their Turkish overlords.

In a curious form of literary colonialism, European travel writers of the late eighteenth and early nineteenth centuries incited Greeks to rebel against their Ottoman rulers and regain the democratic freedom that was their ancestral right, while at the same time claiming the land of Greece as a *natural* part of the western European inheritance. The effects of European philhellenism were to foster a nationalistic myth of continuity with an idealized past, and to encourage a national chauvinism that refused to allow a non Greek-speaking state to call itself Macedonia. The philhellenic legacy caused the Greeks it affected most, that is the most educated class, to view their own Ottoman and Byzantine past as culturally inferior. Through the prism of philhellenism, some aspects of modern Greek music, poetry, architecture, and language were seen as insufficiently "Hellenic." This caused a sort of cultural schizophrenia, causing Greeks to see themselves, at times, as barbarians in their own land.

Two recurrent themes of philhellenic literature are the sense of déjà vu on first sight of the landscape of Greece, and the male traveler's satisfaction with the appearance of Greek women, who seem to fulfill his desire to recapture ancient Greece entire, perfect, and populated with Hellenes. On visiting Greece for the first time in 1788, Thomas Watkins reported that…"the general appearance of the country was the same as ever, but alas! How changed is Athens." On the island of Melos, he finds the women "well-made and beautiful…They are uncommonly full in the bosom, reminding me of Homer's descriptive epithet *bathukolpos*, and their loose and airy manner of clothing themselves heightens that voluptuous appearance for which they have ever been distinguished."

Bosom

(Gail Holst-Warhaft)

A generous word, bosom,
firmly curved as a cello,
or carved on a prow, fulsome
under folds of black taffeta

marking breath's rise and fall,
barometer of love's storms.
How could the be-all
and begin-all of desire

be a thirty-six inch bust?
How could breasts spread one
by one on plastic and crushed
in a scanner be objects of desire?

As for boobs, they sound
like children's toys. Imagine
Homer's women not deep-
bosomed but deep-boobed!

With the discoveries of Bronze Age Crete and Mycenae, the focus of philhellenes was temporarily shifted from Athens, but the myth of Greece as the cradle of European civilization continued to be a common literary motif, often employed by writers to elevate their own self-image. More than a century after Byron's first visit to Greece, an American writer stopped at a little village to get a drink after visiting the ruins of Knossos:

The contrast between the past and the present was tremendous, as though the secret of life had been lost. The men who gathered around me took on the appearance of uncouth savages. They were friendly and hospitable, but by comparison with the Minoans, they were like neglected domestic animals. I am not thinking of the comforts they lacked...I am thinking now of the lack of the those essential elements of life which make possible a real society of human beings...when a miserable Greek village, such as the one I am speaking of, and the counterparts of which we have seen by the thousand in America, embellishes its meager, stultified life by the adoption of a telephone, radio, automobile, tractor, etc., the meaning of the word communal becomes so fantastically distorted that one begins to wonder what is meant by the phrase 'human society.' There is nothing human about these sporadic agglomerations of beings; they are beneath any known level of life which this globe has known. They are less in every way than the pygmies who are truly nomadic and move in filthy freedom with delicious security.

The only thing that redeemed Henry Miller's visit to the Cretan village was the sight of a woman with a vase on her shoulder who had "the pose and grace of a figure on an ancient frieze."

Modern Greek writers may not have been so crudely snobbish as Miller, but they felt they were the guardians of a Hellenic spirit that it was their duty to uphold. From his first major cycle of poems to his Nobel Prize acceptance speech and his reluctant condemnation of the military regime of 1967-74, George Seferis's work was dedicated to the establishment of a vision of calm, resigned Hellenism compatible with what he considered to be the realities of post-Smyrna Greece. His vision not only necessitated the devaluing of the only other poet who had achieved international renown, Constantine Cavafy, but of those poets Seferis saw as nihilist, narrowly political, or in any way inadequate to the task of transmitting his brand of neohellenism.

Cavafy's preference for the post-classical moment, for the Hellenism of the diaspora, where the distinction between Greek and barbarian, pagan and Christina is constantly blurred, was antithetical to the project of recovering a Eurocentric neo-Hellenic, literary identity. It is hardly surprising he should have remained an outsider. Interesting, how frequently "Waiting for the Barbarians" has been invoked by foreign writers, particularly during the 1967-74 dictatorship, when it evoked an image of the Greeks at the mercy of their own barbaric government. Cavafy himself lived beyond the borders of the new Greek state, and the city that inspired him had always embraced a great mixture of cultures. His brand of Hellenism, proud as it may have been, was neither naïve nor ethnocentric. If ever a Greek writer was liberated from the burden of philhellenic expectations, it was Cavafy.

Περιμένοντας τους Βαρβάρους.

Τι περιμένουμε στην αγορά συναθροισμένοι;

Είναι οι βάρβαροι να φθάσουν σήμερα.

— Γιατί μέσα στην Σύγκλητο μια τέτοια απραξία;
Τι κάθοντ᾽ οι Συγκλητικοί και δεν νομοθετούνε;

Γιατί οι βάρβαροι θα φθάσουν σήμερα.
Τι νόμους πια θα κάμουν οι Συγκλητικοί;
Οι βάρβαροι σαν έλθουν θα νομοθετήσουν.

—Γιατί ο αυτοκράτωρ μας τόσο πρωί σηκώθη,
και κάθεται στης πόλεως την πιο μεγάλη πύλη
στον θρόνο επάνω, επίσημος, φορώντας την κορώνα;

Γιατί οι βάρβαροι θα φθάσουν σήμερα.
Κι ο αυτοκράτωρ περιμένει να δεχθεί
τον αρχηγό τους. Μάλιστα ετοίμασε
για να τον δώσει μια περγαμηνή. Εκεί
τον έγραψε τίτλους πολλούς κι ονόματα.

— Γιατί οι δυο μας ύπατοι κ᾽ οι πραίτορες εβγήκαν
σήμερα με τες κόκκινες, τες κεντημένες τόγες·
γιατί βραχιόλια φόρεσαν με τόσους αμεθύστους,
και δαχτυλίδια με λαμπρά, γυαλιστερά σμαράγδια·
γιατί να πιάσουν σήμερα πολύτιμα μπαστούνια
μ᾽ ασήμια και μαλάματα έκτακτα σκαλιγμένα;

Waiting for the Barbarians

Constantine Cavafy (trans. G. Holst-Warhaft)

—What are we waiting for, gathered here in the agora?

The barbarians are expected today.

—Why such idleness in the Senate?
Why are the Senators sitting there, passing no laws?

Because the barbarians are coming today.
What laws would the senators pass?
The barbarians are the ones who'll pass laws.

—Why did our emperor get up so early,
and why is he sitting in state on his throne
at the largest gate of the city, wearing his crown?

Because the barbarians are coming today
and the emperor's waiting to receive their leader.
He's even had a scroll prepared to give him.
It has lots of titles, lots of names written it.

—Why have our two consuls and praetors come out today
wearing their scarlet, embroidered robes?
Why have they put on bracelets with so many amethysts,
rings glinting with brilliant emeralds?
Why do they carry elegant canes
superbly worked in silver and gold?

Γιατί οι βάρβαροι θα φθάσουν σήμερα·
και τέτοια πράγματα θαμπώνουν τους βαρβάρους.

—Γιατί κ' οι άξιοι ρήτορες δεν έρχονται σαν πάντα
να βγάλουνε τους λόγους τους, να πούνε τα δικά τους;

Γιατί οι βάρβαροι θα φθάσουν σήμερα·
κι αυτοί βαρυούντ' ευφράδειες και δημηγορίες.

— Γιατί ν' αρχίσει μονομιάς αυτή η ανησυχία
κ' η σύγχυσις. (Τα πρόσωπα τι σοβαρά που εγίναν).
Γιατί αδειάζουν γρήγορα οι δρόμοι κ' η πλατέες,
κι όλοι γυρνούν στα σπίτια τους πολύ συλλογισμένοι;

Γιατί ενύχτωσε κ' οι βάρβαροι δεν ήλθαν.
Και μερικοί έφθασαν απ' τα σύνορα,
και είπανε πως βάρβαροι πια δεν υπάρχουν.

Και τώρα τι θα γένουμε χωρίς βαρβάρους.
Οι άνθρωποι αυτοί ήσαν μια κάποια λύσις.

Because the barbarians are coming today
and such things dazzle the barbarians.

—Why don't our distinguished orators come out as usual
to make their speeches, say what they always say?

Because the barbarians are coming today
and they're tired of eloquence and public speeches.

—Why this sudden uneasiness, this confusion?
(How serious people's faces have become).
Why are the streets and squares emptying so fast?
Why is everyone heading for home, lost in thought?

Because night has fallen and the barbarians haven't arrived.
And some, who've come from the border, say
there are no barbarians left.

And what will become of us without barbarians?
Those people were a sort of solution.

Waiting for the Europeans

    (Gail Holst-Warhaft)

What are they waiting for in the parliament?

Their suits are Italian, their shoes made in Spain;
their ties are tied despite the heat.
Cars with tinted windows have left
for the airport with sirens screaming and a crowd
has gathered in the square with placards in hand.

Why is the parliament so quiet today?
The Europeans are coming and no-one knows
what gifts they bring. (Greeks know
how dangerous gifts can be for a city).

Why are our leaders stopping at the museum?
Because the Europeans like those things.
They enjoy seeing our glorious ruins.

Why are the protesters leaving the square
placards in hand? Because they've heard

the Europeans left without an agreement
and what will happen without an agreement?

Those Europeans were a sort of solution.

The western powers who helped Greece win independence from the Turks demanded a role in governing the new nation. The 17 year-old Bavarian Prince Otho imposed on the Greeks by the allies, arrived with his own courtiers and troops. Together with a small group of local leaders, they maintained order by a mixture of force and corruption that laid the foundations for a long-lasting climate of political behavior in Greece. Otho's popularity waxed and waned with his Greek subjects in response to international events, and shortly after he was ousted by his dissatisfied subjects, they turned to another prince, this time a Dane, to assume the throne. Independence was always conditional in Greece. It was a small, poor country, at the mercy of larger powers. It had its moment of glory at the beginning of World War II, during the Albanian Campaign, but it lasted a very short time.

*　　*　　*

It was Palm Sunday, a gloomy beginning to the Easter celebration, but there was a sense of unreality in the capital, as if the recent successes of the army might be repeated. The sides of the Acropolis were sprinkled with red poppies and white daisies, the little chapel on Lykavitos hill shone like a candle on a cake, housewives larded their winter clothes with moth-balls and put them away for the following year.

"Down with the house-painter!" people shouted in the streets with a smile. "Down with Hitler!"

The new leader of the Greek nation had no idea what to do and committed suicide. The king, always a dubious figure in Greece, took control of what was now a rapidly leaking tub of state.

Easter 1941 was a disaster. The Greeks fought bravely in the north, but news from the battlefields was uniformly glum. The Germans had taken most of the towns in the north and were closing in on the capital. The annual broadcast of the Easter service from the cathedral was interrupted by sobs from the congregation and the bishop's voice wavered.

For the first and last time in modern Greek history, the celebration of the Resurrection, the joyous midnight climax of the Orthodox Church year, was postponed until the following morning.

British army units, many of them familiar with the Classics and sentimental about the Spartans, took a temporary stand on the hallowed ground of Themopylae, but did not fight, like Leonidas, to the death. A new Prime Minister, Tsouderos, was appointed but he soon left Athens with the king, the royal family, and the rest of the government, for Crete.

In the streets of the capital the mood had changed. Greek soldiers fleeing the Germans in the North, had taken off their uniforms and were slowly making their way back to Athens on foot. Some roamed the streets in their pyjamas, begging for food. The people began to comprehend that the resistance was finished, that they had been abandoned by their own government. On the 27th of April Athens was deserted. A German convoy of advance troops entered the city unopposed. Three days later they took over the radio and began broadcasting in Greek to the citizens of Athens. On the same day they raised the swastika on the Acropolis. In the center of the city, apartments and rooms were requisitioned by the German officers and administrators. The displaced citizens moved in reluctantly with neighbors or set out for their summer houses in the villages.

The mainland may have fallen, but there was a glimmer of hope in Crete, where 27, 500 British and Allied troops remained, determined to hold the island as a last bastion dividing the German army in Greece from Rommel's North African regiments, and from the Suez Canal. Despite their anger and dismay, those Greeks who remained loyal to the King were comforted that he and his government were still on Greek soil and that more than a thousand Greek soldiers, however ill-equipped and poorly trained, were fighting alongside the British.

Hope died only after the most unlikely invasion of the war. No country had ever been invaded by parachute before May 20th, 1941. The invasion of Crete caught the British and Greek troops by surprise. Early in the morning the landing began with a heavy bombardment aimed at the planes and anti-aircraft guns installed at the airports. Then the sky filled with what looked like thistledown floating slowly to earth. Two thousand men jumped in the first wave, each one armed only with four hand grenades, a pistol and a knife. At Hania, New Zealand troops hidden in the olive groves picked off hundreds of them as they drifted earthwards in the warm currents of air. The German High Command received no word of the heavy casualties because the leaders of the advance wave were dead, and a second wave followed as planned.

It was mid-afternoon, and by now all the forces on the ground were ready for the black figures that fell slowly and helplessly downwards. Of the twenty-two thousand men who were dropped, five-and-a-half thousand were killed before they reached the ground, including the commanders of both groups. "Operation Mercury," designed to capture the airfields, towns, and ports of Crete in a single day, had failed completely. Hitler was so appalled by the German casualties that he did not order another airborne invasion for the remainder of the war. Losses on the other side were heavy too, and the surviving Germans, backed up by reinforcements, eventually managed to establish control over the island. The British Army withdrew to Egypt, leaving a small force of Australians and New Zealanders behind. The Greek king and his government followed the British and spent the war years comfortably ensconced in Egypt.

One tenth of the Greek population died during the remainder of the war, most of them from starvation, the rest were killed in reprisal for their acts of resistance. Of the once proud Jewish communities of Greece, more than 90 percent were killed in transports or in concentration camps.

*   *   *

As the first summer of the Occupation passed and winter approached, the Germans began requisitioning food and fuel to send home. In the countryside it was easy to hide small quantities of oil or flour, but in Athens inflation soared and bread soon disappeared from the stores. The only way to find food was to barter whatever you had for it. On the 28th of October, the first anniversary of Metaxas's famous "No!" there were demonstrations in the streets of the capital. Flowers and wreaths were piled at the statue of the first great poet of modern Greece, Dionysios Solomos, in the National Gardens.

November came and a cold December. Frost-bitten war veterans and small children roamed the streets where people fainted from hunger and begged for food. Girls of eleven and twelve were dressed up by their mothers in whatever clothing they could spare and offered to Italian sailors in exchange for food. Babies were left on the doorsteps of the richer apartment buildings. So many people died each night that carts were sent to collect the bodies from the streets of the city every morning. During the first winter of the Occupation a thousand people died of hunger every day in Athens and Piraeus. In January and February, the daily toll of the dead rose to two thousand. By the end of the winter, 150,000 people in Athens and Piraeus had died. The International Red Cross reported that this was a higher figure than in any other occupied country in Europe, with the exception of Poland.

There was no wood for coffins, no clothing to dress the dead. Those who could afford to rented coffins but mostly the dead were buried in large, open pits. Among the piles of bodies waiting for burial, those that were clothed were soon stripped. Electricity and heating were often cut; all public transportation stopped. On Sina Street in the fashionable quarter of Kolonaki, a horse died in a pool of blood. A crowd gathered around it waiting to dismember the body. On Massalias Street, a photographer recorded a heap of bodies waiting for burial. The Germans had succeeded in starving the Greeks into submission during that first winter, but anti-German sentiment was so high that acts of sabotage and resistance began in the countryside. They were savagely punished, but they satisfied a need for action.

One night, at the end of May, two teenage boys climbed the wall behind Anafiotika in the darkness and tore down the swastika flying over the Acropolis. Who can say what effect such acts of daring have? Some credit the two boys with starting the Greek resistance movement. Given the conditions in Athens that year, perhaps the vanished flag was enough. At any rate the two boys became heroes in the eyes of the Greeks that summer, while the resistance that would tear Greece apart took shape.

During the last months of the war, as the Italians capitulated and a German defeat became a matter of time, the resistance grew bolder, especially in the north, and German reprisals had a quality of desperation to them. The names of two villages have become synonymous with the savagery of that last summer. In Distomo, three hundred people of all ages were shot and burned to death after a German patrol was fired on by guerrillas. In Hortiati, women and children were herded into the local bakery and burned after a similar attack. By July of 1944, 879 Greek villages had been totally destroyed. The Germans refused to let peasants work land, and commandeered their houses. By August the Red Cross reported that forty percent of rural population had lost their homes and many were living in the open. Tuberculosis became rampant and malnutrition was so severe in Epirus that many children suffered from temporary blindness.

The city of Salonika was home to most of Greece's Jewish population. Many of them fought beside their Christian neighbors in the Albanian mountains. When the Germans occupied the city, Jews were not singled out for special treatment until July, 1942, when Jewish men were ordered to assemble in Eleftherios Square and made to hop like frogs and perform other humiliations, beaten and doused with water. Two days later, those who obeyed a new summons were drafted into work camps from which most of them never returned. Why Salonika's Jewish community stayed put, instead of joining the Greek resistance in the mountains, or simply fleeing to the Italian zone, is a mystery that can only be explained by the behavior of the chief rabbi of Salonika, Zevi Koretz.

Herded into a poor quarter near the railway station, the Jews were told that they would be transported to work camps in Poland. They were even issued a check each for 600 zlotys by the Gestapo. Koretz, who had been detained by the Gestapo while on a trip to Athens in 1941 and transported to Austria, where he was held and interrogated for eight months, was either a willing instrument of the Germans, or monumentally naïve. Even once the transports had begun he continued to discourage his community from joining the resistance or use any other avenue of escape. By 1943 only five hundred of the estimated 56,000 Jews that were living in Salonika when the war broke out remained. They owed their lives to the fact that they retained their Spanish citizenship. The old and distinguished communities of northern Greece had disappeared in a single summer: Kavalla, Kastoria, Serres, Drama, Xanthi....Then it was the turn of the five thousand Greek Jews who lived on the islands. The thoroughness of the destruction was astonishing. Only a month before they withdrew from Greece the Nazis rounded up the Jewish communities of Evia, Rhodes, Kos, and Corfu. Almost all of them perished. A physician who performed autopsies for the Nazis at Auschwitz noted:

Last night they burned the Greek Jews from the Mediterranean island of Corfu, one of the oldest communities of Europe. The victims were kept for twenty-seven days without food or water, first in launches, then in sealed cars. When they arrived at Aus-

chwitz's leading platform, the doors were unlocked but no one got out to line up for selection. Half of them were already dead and half in a coma. The entire convoy without exception was sent to number two crematorium.

14. Eros and Katerina

Katerina Anghelaki-Rooke's godfather, Nikos Kazantzakis, was impressed by the poems Katerina wrote as a teenager and sent them to literary friends in Athens. From then on she was established as a figure on the Athenian literary scene. She grew up speaking Russian and French, and has translated Dylan Thomas's *Under Milkwood*, a volume of Seamus Heaney's poems, and (the translation she was proudest of) Pushkin's *Eugene Onegin* into Greek. She won the Greek state prize for poetry. In addition to English, her poems have been translated into French, Polish, Romanian, and Hebrew.

I met her soon after I arrived in Greece and it took me three decades not to be intimidated by her. She was a brilliant linguist, and unforgiving of any errors in the Greek of her foreign friends. Our mistakes, like many other things, made her explode with laughter. She and her husband Rodney drank heavily, but nothing interfered with her writing and translation. I began translating her poems in the 1980's. It took me a much longer time to ask her to translate my poems into Greek.

Katerina, whose father died during the dictatorship, inherited his house on the island of Aigina. She kept a flat in Athens, but her summers and weekends were spent in the two-storied house surrounded by a pistachio orchard that her father had built in the 1930's. Nikos Kazantzakis and his second wife Eleni were living not far away and the two men became friends. Not much has been done to the house since then. Its red walls have acquired the patina of an ancient Chinese bronze. Inside, it cries out for attention, but it still stands solid as the day it was built, behind the port near the old jail. From the terrace, you look over the stiff limbs of the pistachios towards the sea.

Katerina's Athenian friends came to visit. Others ended up moving permanently to the island. In summer, more friends and admirers arrived from England or America, some staying for months. Summer was an endless party, with Katerina talking, telling jokes, laughing, and drinking at the center of it, and her husband Rodney alternating between witty asides and sleep. Dishes piled up in the sink. Beer and ouzo bottles littered the tables. Katerina, who loved the sea, rode her bicycle to swim in the shallow, tepid waters near the port, but even in summer she managed to find a few hours a day to write or translate. Lovers would sometimes be there too. They were accepted as part of the poet's existence, the drug she needed to write, to feel attractive. Shortly after she was born, Katerina had contracted a staphylococcus infection that almost killed her, and left her with a strong limp and a withered arm. Her childhood was overshadowed by a series of surgeries in Switzerland to try to straighten her limbs. Perhaps it was what turned her into a worshipper of beauty. Her appetites were large and her love poems are probably the most frankly sexual poems of any Greek poet, male or female. One side of her was hopelessly romantic, tapioca in the hands of her lovers. The intellectual side was as tough as a pomegranate rind.

In a volume called *Contrary Love*, Katerina reveals herself in poetry and prose on facing pages — the lover and the poet, who, in the throes of passion, maintains an ironic detachment, a sureness of herself as an artist, the lover as merely muse.

Katerina Anghelaki-Rooke

Poems from *Contrary Love* by Katerina Anghelaki-Rooke

Ο Τζίτζικας

Μέσα μου χιλιάδες τραγούδια στοιβάζονται καλοκαιρινά. Ανοίγω το στόμα μου και μες στο πάθος μου προσπαθώ να τους βάλω μια σειρά. Τραγουδώ. Άσχημα. Αλλά χάρη στο τραγούδι μου ξεχωρίζω σπό τις φλούδες των κλάδων και από τ'άλλα άφωνα ηχεία της φύσης. Η απέριττη περιβολή μου – γκρίζα κι ασβεστένια — μου αποκλείει κάθε παραφορά αισθητισμού κι έτσι αποκομμένος απ' τα φανταχτερά πανηγύρια του χρόνου, τραγουδάω. Άνοιξη, Πάσχα και βιολέτες, δεν γνωρίζω. Τη μόνη ανάσταση που ξέρω είναι όταν μόλις σηκώνεται κάποιο αεράκι και δροσίζει λίγο τη φοβερή κάψα της ζωής μου. Τότε παύω να ουρλιάζω – ή να τραγουδάω όπως νομίζει ο κόσμος – γιατί το θαύμα μίας δροσιάς μέσα μου βαθιά λέει περισσότερα απ'όλα όσα δημιουργώ να μην πεθάνω από τη ζέστη.

The Cicada

Thousands of summer songs accumulate inside me. I open my mouth and in my passion, try to put them in order. I sing. Badly. But thanks to my song I stand out from the branches and from other voiceless sound-boxes of nature. My simple dress—grey and lime-white—bars me from every excess of aestheticism and so, cut off from the loud annual festival, I sing. Spring, Easter and violets I know nothing of. The only resurrection I know is when a faint breeze just manages to stir and slightly cool the burning heat of my life. Then I stop howling—or, as the world thinks, singing—because the miracle of coolness deep inside me says more than all I create so as not to die of heat.

Η Ζέστη

Στη ζέστη της Ελλάδας
Τα κολλημένα στέρνα μας
Ανάβληζαν νερα΄
Έπινα τον ιδρώτα σου
Μαζί με τα φιλιά σου
Το αχ σου
Στη σκια του πατζουριού.
Την ωρα που ανέβαινε
το άγριο μεσημέρι του τόπου
εφούντωνες και συ
με τα τρελλά τσουλούφια σου
τα θεία τσίνορά σου
το γέλιο σου πολύεδρο
μες στ'αλμυρά πρίσματα του πάθους.
Στην τόση λάβρα
στην τόση ακινησία,
με μόνο ίσκιο πάνο μας
το μαύρο πεπρωμένο,
τα σκίτσα της υπαρξής μας
έμοιαζαν μ'εξίσωση εντόμων.
Κακοφορμίζει ο Αύγουστος
σαν ανοιχτή πληγή
και τα τζιτζίκια αστείρευτα
θυμίζουν πάλι τον ποιντή
στου ποιήματος το τέλος.
Άπνοια...
Η μύγα σχολαστικά τα πάντα π'ασχημίζει

The Heat

In the heat of Greece
our chests, stuck together,
oozed water;
I drank your sweat
with your kisses
your sigh
in the shade of the shutter.
At the hour when
the angry noontide of the land rose up
you swelled too
with your crazy curls,
your divine eyelashes,
your laughter multifaceted
in the salty prisms of passion.
In such blistering heat
in such stillness
with the only shadow over us
the black certainty of fate,
the scrawls of our existence
resembled the equations of insects.
August festers
like an open wound
and the relentless cicadas
remind one of the poet
at the end of the poem.
Not a breath of air...
The fly, pedantic in all it defiles,

εκάθησε στο πέος σου
και τρώει το χυμό σου.
Περνάει με το μεγάφωνο
αυτός με τα καρπούζια.
Το μεσημέρι πέφτει
στα πόδια μου
σαν κεφάλη κομμένη.

sits on your penis
drinking your sap.
A megaphone passes,
the watermelon man.
The afternoon falls
at my feet
like a cut-off head.

Τα Σπιρτόξυλα

Ο Γκιούλιβερ
Που ξύπνησε μες στον αγρο, στο χώμα καρφομένος σαν τα κρινάκια,
στερεωμένος όπως τα στάχυα, βιδωμένος ως κι απ'τις πιό λεπτές
τρίχες της μύτης του, κολλημένος σαν έντομο στου εντυμολόγου το
τεφτέρι, πανικόβλητος σαν είδε πως ο τεράστιος όγκος του κρμιού
του ήταν το έδαφος για εκατομμύρια μεγαλοφυείς επιχειρήσεις
μικρότατων ανθρώπωνπου με σπιρτόξυλα και κοωστές τον είχαν
καταδικάσει σε ακινησία
είμαι εγώ
με τους λιλιπούτειους παράφορους έρωτές μου με κρατούν δέσμια
της πιο χωμάτινης αντίληψης της ζωής, της πιο περιορισμένης
κίνησης, μιας χαμερπέστατης σύλληψης του ωραίου σαν σώμα που
γδύνεται και ξαπλώνεται κι ουδέποτε ανεβαίνει στους ουρανούς.

Matchsticks

Gulliver

who woke in the field, pinned to the earth like the lilies, fastened like ears of wheat, screwed down even by the finest hairs in his nose, stuck like an insect in an entomologist's notebook, panicking as he saw how the great bulk of his body was the terrain for millions of brilliant enterprises carried out by tiny people who with matchsticks and threads had reduced him to immobility

is me

with my Lilliputian frenzied loves that keep me bound to the most cloddish conception of life, the most constrained movement, to a base apprehension of beauty as a body that undresses and lies down and never rises to the skies.

Το τρίτο καλοκαίρι – η κασταστροφή

Το σπίτι είχε πέσει σε ύπνο γλυκό,
πέτρες πόρτες, μια ψυχή – πουρή
που εσωτερικά πάντα κατοικεί τον εαυτό της
ενώ η κουκουβάγια απέξο σταθερή
υμνεί της νύχτας το βαθύ τέλος.
Ήταν το τρίτο καλοκαίρι,
που φάνηκε το ίδιο μικρό άτομο
ενα πολυδάπανο μέρος της οικουμενικής ομορφιάς,
αυτής που καθορίζει κι ακαθόριστη μένει.
"Ανοίχτε τα μάτια, έλεγαν τα κακά προαισθήματα,
δέστε τις φουντωτής ουρές των ζώων
πως ισχναίνουν στο χρόνο
κι ο, τι λατρέψατε κάτω
απ'τις μανταρινιές
πως ύπουλα διαβαίνουν το κατώφλι."

Κάτι μας φτιάχνει και φτιάχνουμε
τους τοίχους έναν έναν, γύρω γύρω
και στη μέση βάζουμε την εστία
και τη παστάδα, την πορτοκαλάδα
δίπλα στο τραπεζάκι.
Δεν ειν' ιδιοκτησία΄ το φως καλούμε
μέσα να 'μπει, να μιλήσει
για τα νοήματα και τις σκιές
που 'χει συλλάβει να συλλογάται μοναχό του.

The Third Summer — the Catastrophe

from *The Suitors* by Katerina Anghelaki-Rooke

The house had fallen into a sweet sleep,
stone doors, a calcified soul
that always internally inhabits itself
while outside the steadfast owl
praises the deep end of night.
It was the third summer that the same small individual had appeared,
a profligate part of this universal beauty
that defines and remains indefinable.
"Open your eyes," said the evil forebodings,
"look at the bushy tails of the animals,
see how straggly they become with time
and how what you adored under
the mandarin trees
furtively crosses the threshold."

Something makes us and we make
the walls one by one, all around
and in the middle we place the hearth
and the bridal chamber, the orange juice
on the bedside table.
It's not private property; we invite the light
to enter, to talk
about the meanings and the shadow
it has grasped and is contemplating alone.

Μα ξέρουν τα πικρά κι αγιάτρευτα γεράνια
πως κείνο που θρέφει τα σύμβολα
αιώνιας ευαιξίας, θρέφει και τα θεριά με αγριάδα
Καλοσύνες απατηλής οι μέρες του καλοκαιριού
σκληρή ειν' η απλόχωρη ασυνοδοσία του γαλάζιου
κι οι σκέψεις που στο νερό παν να δροσιστούν
μες στο βυθό βουλιάζουν.
Κι αυτή η φύση απρόσκοπτα
ποτέ της δεν πορεύεται στο χρόνο·
ακόμα και στην εκθρότητα στηρίζεται
αν είναι γιά ν'ανθίσει.
Λες καμιά φορά που τίποτα
πιά δεν μεστώνει και 'πάνω στο λουλούδισμα
τα φαρμακώνει όλα η τρέλα.
κι αυτοί που χτυπούν
κι αυτοί που φωτιά βάζουν
ήσαν κάποτε λατρεμένοι·
κάθονται στη σκιά γυμνοί
στη πάνινη καρέκλα
στη μέση τους φορούσαν ζώνη τα φιλιά
με μια λουρίδα της λάτρισσας ευχές
ως τη χωρισιά, εκεί που σμίγουν με φωνές
οι ζήλιες όλες.
Ετσι κι ο καλεσμένος του σώματός μου
αφίνει το δροσερό κάθισμα·
τα δάχτυλα που ευφάνταστα ακουμπούσαν
στο μπανιαρό γίνονται ορνιού νύχια
σε ζώω κακό μεταμορφώνεται ο έρωτας.

But the bitter, incurable geraniums know
that what nourishes the symbols
of eternal well-being, also feeds the beasts with ferocity.
Deceptive kindness, these summer days,
the expansive unity of blue is harsh
and the thoughts that go to cool themselves in the water
sink into the depths.
And this unimpeded nature
never goes forward in time;
it even braces itself in enmity
if it's about to flower.
Sometimes you say that nothing
ripens anymore and at the time of flowering
madness poisons it all.
And those who beat people
or set things on fire
were worshipped once;
they would sit naked in the shade
on the canvas chair
wearing a belt of kisses round their waists
with the devotee's string of blessings
down to the crack, there where all jealousies
merge with cries.
And so the guest of my body
leaves the cool seat;
the fingers that playfully rested
on the bathing suit become vulture's claws,
love is transformed into an evil beast.

Νύχτα μοχθηρή. Άλλοτε μόνο αγιόκλημα
κι η γλώσσα του βαθιά μπηγμένη
στη πηγή της ευφροσύνης.
Τώρα στο σπίτι φύσηξ' όλεθρος
τα έπιπλα μανιάσαν, σηκώθηκαν
στις μήτες, στις γωνιες· στις στρογγυλάδες τους
κι ύστερα κατρακύλησαν
στο βάραθρο του ονείρου·
μαζί κι εγώ, εν' άψυχο κασόνι
έπεσα, κομματιάστηκα
με τα καρφιά μου όλα στο πάτωμα,

τα δόντια σπαρμένα.

Spiteful night. Once only the honeysuckle

and his tongue dipped deep

into the well of delight.

Now catastrophe blew through the house,

the crazed furniture rose

on its edges, its corners, its curves

then tumbled into the chasm of dream;

I fell too, came to pieces,

a lifeless crate

with my nails all over the floor

my teeth scattered.

15. Greeks, Old and New

Poems by Gail Holst-Warhaft

Poets' Café

For Katerina Anghelaki-Rooke

An addict trails her dusty skirts
past tables where poets still meet
for coffee. My poet friend averts

her eye. She has enough to pay
for a slice of cheesecake, sweet distraction
from the ouzo of many a yesterday.

The café's full of famous friends
lounging in sunlit sidewalk chairs.
Coffee's a luxury, but one pretends

things are unchanged. An Albanian woman
helps my friend remember to eat;
she used to live on words and young men.

For years on her island she wrote of absence,
of her aging body's greed for beauty
and beauty's endless need for reverence.

Now she writes of deepening loss,
purple ink on the page still faithful
to the musky god she worshipped, Eros.

Goddess on the Half Shell

Scallop, comb, and cunt: one Greek word
served for the shell whose open halves
revealed the goddess of love, Aphrodite
kneeling between its pin-striped valves,

the comb whose teeth the scored
shell mimicked, and the soft elastic
flesh. On the shell's fringe
a row of eyes glittered like a necklace

for a princess or the goddess grown inside
the closed wings of the *pecten jacobeus*.
Queen of the beach, Andipatros called her,
and of the bedroom's salt exchange.

She led ships safely to shore
and hearts to shipwreck on her shell's edge.
"Don't break my spirit!" cried Sappho
knowing She had the power.

Baubo

When Demeter reached Eleusis
the women in charge of the mysteries
plied her with food and drink
but she was still sick with grief
for her lost daughter, Persephone,
and the earth stayed cold and dark.

The women wanted Spring
to bud the almonds, dust
the earth green, wake
lust in their chilly limbs.
If only they could make her
take a little food, a little wine.

But her tears spilled down
and the women grew tired
of consoling. One called Baubo
had an inspiration: she lifted her skirt,
and out of the grieving goddess
came a laugh that summoned Spring.

Euridice

In the underworld you age fast.
Fortunately candles are kind.
In the halls where pomegranate seeds
stained our lips red, we saw
the smudged outlines in the mirror
of a beauty we knew had left us.
You came for a girl who trod
lightly in the wedding dance,
not for a shade, a shard
of a wife. Your music charmed us all
　—women, cats, even the Dark Lord —
until he set me free to follow.
"Don't look at her," he told you,
not because I might vanish.
One look, he knew, would be enough
to kill the song beauty prompts.

Roundtrip

Love led him to hell and back;
song bought his roundtrip ticket.

He thought his lyre would grant him company
for the journey back but before he left

it was all decided. "If he charms us"
Hades drawled, he can have his wife

… for a while," and they laughed. Eurydice
didn't bother to pack her bags.

They heard him when he was still far off
on the path that tilted down towards them

and froze in languorous attitudes, hand
half-way to mouth, knees slack.

Blood rushed up their tired veins;
it was as if the sun had come.

By the light of his music they saw themselves
as morning-after revelers do:

uncouth creatures of the night, not fit
to be seen in such a brilliant glare.

Missing Possibilities

for David Curzon

My life fills with missing persons
as it empties of possibilities.
On one side, dead weight,
on the other a bronze Eros
hangs suspended, his wings
too small to counteract
gravity's pull.

16. Aristophanes in a Basement

In the winter of 1977-78, the small club "Rigas," in the Plaka district overflowed with customers each night. The cream of Greece's intelligentsia was there – students, novelists, poets, journalists, musicians, film directors — watching a musical version of Aristophanes' *Acharnians*. Katerina Anghelaki, my poet friend, had already seen the show and told me it was brilliant. I must come with her to see it. We met on a side-street in Plaka that I'd never noticed before. The basement club was already nearly full, but we squeezed onto chairs and ordered ouzo as the crowd of Athenians pushed their way into every spare corner of the room. Dozens were left standing along the walls, and since most of them were smoking I hated to think what would happen if a fire broken out. Writers who knew Katerina called out to her and a desperate waiter fought his way to our table as we waited for the man of the hour to appear.

I had seen him before, not long after the coup d'état. He was singing in a bar off Adrianou Street. With his long, lank hair and horn-rimmed glasses, his guitar and angry lyrics, he would have fitted in just as well at a café in San Francisco or at a Paris *boite*. Nothing about his style was Greek. There were echoes of Jacques Brel, Georges Brassens, Bob Dylan, but in Athens he was something new. When his first album came out, Dionysis Savvopoulos was hailed as an original song-writer and a sharp social commentator, and he soon became popular, especially in the intellectual circles of Athens and Salonika. Because people were talking about him I'd gone to hear him one night, but aside from the incongruity of his appearance in Athens, and the fierce roughness of his voice, I was not too excited. After I listened to his L.P., *Truck*, (goo.gl/E76oKF) I changed my mind. Here was someone writing about new subjects, about prostitutes, performing monkeys, teenage girls and their small urban dreams:

Δυο δυο πέρασαν πέρασαν νάτα δυο κορίτσια
όλο ντρέπονται ντρέπονται όλο τα κορίτσια

τα κορίτσια τα κορίτσια δύο δύο βιαστικά
στρίβουν από τη γωνία για να μπουν στο σινεμά
στέκουν πίσω από το τζάμι και ζητάνε παγωτό
τα κορίτσια που 'χουν γίνει δεκατέσσερα χρονώ

Σε λευκώματα όμορφα γράφουν τα κορίτσια
πριν πλαγιάσουνε κλείνουν κλειδώνουν τα κορίτσια

στον καθρέφτη στον καθρέφτη κάθε βράδυ στα κρυφά
βλέπουνε να μεγαλώνουν μ' ένα φόβο στην καρδιά
τη μαμά τους τη ρωτάνε κάθε τόσο μια φορά
τα κορίτσια που περνάνε δύο δύο βιαστικά

Περιμένουνε στη στάση σαν σχολάνε απ' τ' Αγγλικά
ο συμμαθητής της μοιάζει κάποιον γόη του σινεμά

Πόσο όμορφα όμορφα βλέπεις τα κορίτσια
πόσο άτυχα άτυχα βλέπεις τα κορίτσια
την ασχήμια των γονιών τους θα πληρώσουνε σκληρά
κάποια μέρα σα χαμένα θα σταθούν στην εκκλησιά
η μαμά τους θα δακρύζει-συγγενείς πεθερικά
τα κορίτσια τα καημένα κι ούτε λέξη πια γι' αυτά

There they go, two by two, the girls,
all embarrassed, see them? The girls.

Two by two the girls in a hurry
turning the corner to the cinema.
They stand at the corner and ask for ice-cream
the girls who have only just turned fourteen.

In bright white notebooks they write, the girls,
before they sleep with doors locked tight, the girls.

Before the mirror in secret each night
they watch themselves grow up in fright
each month telling their mothers their worries
two by two the girls in a hurry.

After English class they wait on the bus-stop
their classmate looks like some movie heartthrob.

How beautiful they look to you, the girls,
how unfortunate they look to you, the girls.
Their parents' ugliness will cost them dear;
one day in church they'll stand in fear,
their mothers will cry with all the in-laws
of the poor little girls, and not a word more.

During the dictatorship, Savvopoulos's popularity sky-rocketed. With Theodorakis and many of Greece's leading cultural figures in exile, a new generation of Greeks was growing up. Fed on a diet of military marches, Christian hymns, and folk music, they were attracted to everything foreign, especially rock music. It was the sixties, after all, and the first student riot of the dictatorship occurred in Athens at a showing of the film *Woodstock*. Savvopoulos quickly adapted his music to the tastes of the times, hiring young rock and jazz musicians to play with him and writing songs that reflected the prevailing mood of disillusionment and cynicism. His young audience was born in the city, not in the village, and came of age during a puritanical dictatorship. It was not surprising that they responded to his songs, which reflected the reality of urban Greece in the late nineteen-sixties and early seventies:

Όπου κοιτάζω να κοιτάζεις
όλη η Ελλάδα ατέλειωτη παράγκα
παράγκα, παράγκα, παράγκα του χειμώνα
κι εσύ μιλάς σαν πτώμα.

Look wherever I look
the whole of Greece a hovel,
hovel, hovel of winter
and you talk like a dead-beat.

Όχι, όχι αυτό δεν είναι τραγούδι
Είναι η τρύπια στέγη μιας παράγκας
Είναι η γόπα που μάζεψε ένας μάγκας
Κι ο χαφιές που μας ακολουθεί.

No, no, this isn't a song,
it's the leaking roof of a hovel,
the roach picked up by a bum
and the informer on our tails.

I was still something of a purist about Greek music. I missed the
sounds and rhythms I associated with Greece, and I found the borrow-
ings from western popular music irritating. Wedged into a smoke-filled
basement with Katerina chatting to half of Athens, I wondered if this
show that everyone was talking about might offer something that was
both new and Greek.

The Acharnians turned out to be an artistic coup as brilliant in its
way as Aristophanes' original. Despite – perhaps because – of the fact
that one of its main targets was Theodorakis, I was fascinated. The au-
dience was full of intellectuals, as Katerina pointed out, and it was not
surprising. To fully appreciate the performance, you needed to know
not only your classical Greek original, but how Aristophanes' comedy
played off a tragedy by Euripides, and how both were related to a precise
political moment in the Athens of the Peloponnesian War. I understood
only half of the script that night, but I had the feeling that this was how
Aristophanes should be done. The dictatorship was still a raw wound,
the post dictatorship malaise had settled in. Athens was in the mood
for a comedy, one with sharp teeth, and here was a capering clown who
delivered a strange brew of music, poetry and satire as relevant to 1977
Athens as its model had been to the same city of 425 BC.

Aristophanes was already in big trouble when he produced his *Acha-
rnians* that year. In an earlier play called *Babylonians*, he had criticized
several state offices and politicians. In response, Cleon had indicted him
for wrong-doing and hubris. Instead of backing down, Aristophanes
wrote the most political play ever staged in Athens. The *Acharnians* not
only attacks the same individuals and institutions the playwright had

attacked in his previous play, but the hero, Dikeopolis, commits an act of treason by making peace, in the middle of the Peloponnesian War, with the Spartans. The play parodies all the major democratic institutions of the city: the assembly, the law court and the symposium, and it does so by borrowing some affecting rhetoric from Euripidean tragedy. Euripides had written a tragedy that does not survive about the mythical character Telephus. Most of what we know about the tragedy comes from Aristophanes, who helped himself to pieces of Euripides' drama to set up his own satirical comedy.

The stage of the small nightclub was minimally decorated and looked somewhere between a side-show tent at a country fair and a children's birthday party. As he introduced the show, Savvopoulos hopped onstage waving a tambourine in one hand and holding the microphone in the other. Declaring himself "The Musician," he immediately began to comment on the text, talking to his audience in the same conspiratorial tone as his ancient predecessor had done.

The Athenians, he noted, had established democracy, but were now its victims in a town where "everything has become words, politics, garbage spilled on the road, plague, starvation and epidemics." This immediately got a laugh from the audience, infuriated by incessant garbage strikes and long-winded speeches from the political parties struggling to establish themselves in the aftermath of the dictatorship. As the show unfolded, the parallels with modern Athens seemed too good to be true. The grimy, solemn charcoal-burners who had fought at the Battle of Marathon and so had impeccable credentials, were a perfect parallel for the Old Left of Greece, the partisans who'd fought against the German Occupation, and later on the Left side of the Civil War.

Like Aristophanes, the new master of ceremonies at a comic festival addressed us from the stage, drawing us into the fun, luring us to his side. He never laughed himself, but his deadpan attacks on the war-mongering charcoal-burners and on Athenian politicians soon had the audience rocking in their seats. Katerina, who has the loudest laugh of anyone in Athens, guffawed and spluttered beside me. "Brilliant! Fantastic!" she called. I was stretching my ears to take in the fast patter of words and had no time to laugh. The high point of the evening came when the hero, Dikeopolis, laid his head on the butcher's block and pleaded his defense.

If he was to be the solution to Athens' problems, the hero must demolish his competition. But first he'd have to borrow a costume that would make him a pathetic figure: some rags and a hump. The addition of the hump linked him with the hero of the Greek shadow puppet theater, the wily and beloved Karaghiozis. He knew exactly where to go to find his rags: to the "Super-artist" of the day: Euripides. As Savvopoulos explained to the audience, "It's a peculiar scene, because although Dikeopolis begs for the rags and rhetoric that the chorus is so fond of, at the same time he mocks them!"

Not moving from his microphone, he began a dialogue with Euripides, playing both parts. "Eh Euripides, can you lend me that tragic melody 'with a dagger at the bone and a strap at the neck'...."

A small explosion from Katerina sprayed the table. The rest of the audience snickered delightedly. The lines were from the song Theodorakis sang himself at every concert after the dictatorship fell, a setting of Ritsos's poem "Don't Weep for the Greek Spirit." Aristophanes had borrowed from Euripidean tragedy to make his attack on the Athens of his day. Savvopoulos borrowed from the quasi-sacred song of protest, a combination of Theodorakis and Ritsos, to do the same. The all-out attack on Theodorakis was just heating up.

Euripides, please, a tatter or a rag –
let begging be my stage-prop,
put the cap on top
of my head, fly exile's flag...

A pregnant pause. Savvopoulos flung his arms out wide…
"*The Debt!*"

For months, billboards all over Greece had been advertising *The Debt*, a two-volume compilation of Theodorakis's journals and writings during the dictatorship. The cover photograph showed the composer conducting, his arms flung wide. The audience roared.

It was funny, but it was a shot below the belt. Unlike a lot of Greece's intellectuals during the period of the dictatorship, Theodorakis and Ritsos did not choose exile or wear it as a flag. Ritsos was under house arrest on the island of Samos; Theodorakis was jailed and exiled in Greece and abroad. Was Savvopoulos, whose very brief stint in jail was followed by a flourishing career under the dictatorship, jealous?

The moment passes, the hero succeeds with the help of his borrowed rags and the rhetoric of tragedy. The pathos that Theodorakis and Ritsos stood for still has the capacity to move the chorus it seems. The fun goes on despite the attempts of a pompous General Lamarchus to spoil the party in the name of militaristic patriotism. The still-warm memories of the dictatorship have given the exchange between the comic peace-maker and his humorless opponent a pithy zip, and the triumph of the peace camp is celebrated with wine and song.

The man who seemed to be an outsider in the old world of Greek music, a voice against the system, was now appealing to his audience to join him in his break with the old leftist icons. The move was prophetic. Savvopoulos, who opposed the dictatorship and was seen as a leftist himself, would gradually move the right of Greek politics, praising the army, the church, the very icons the Colonels upheld. The party we were attending was one for initiates, I realized, for the neo-conservatives of Greece. It would lead in a direction many of his present audience would not want to follow, but for the moment Dionysis Savvopoulos was crowning himself the Dionysos of his private festival.

"Brilliant!" Katerina shouted again, as we shouldered our way out onto the street. The faces around us were still smiling, and there was already a line outside the club for the second show. I wished I hadn't missed so much of the fast talk and vowed to see the show again. I never imagined how often I would see it.

In the 1970's there were few musicians in Athens who could play the *santouri*, or hammered dulcimer. The santouri-player who performed in the *Acharnians* had another commitment and had given notice to Savvopoulos. Savvopoulos liked the particular shimmering timbre of the santouri in his band and wondered how to replace it. One of his friends suggested he might use a harpsichord.

Savvopoulos's friend asked me to meet him at the club the next night. Between shows, we would go backstage to talk to the great man. Savvopoulos was sitting in his dressing-room, a glass of whiskey in one hand, surrounded by admirers and friends. He wore a silk robe, beads of sweat covering his startlingly white face, damp strands of hair hanging limply to his shoulders. Every remark he made caused a ripple of laughter around the cramped room. He made no effort to stand as he greeted me. Nor did he shake my hand.

"Could you play something like the santouri part?"

"I think so," I lied.

"You'd have to come to learn it. There's no music. You play by ear?"

I wanted to learn more about this man and his music. I wasn't going to admit I had any doubts about his music. I had the feeling that in this world of the side-show, everything depended on my own self-confidence.

"Yes," I said briskly. He nodded as if to indicate that the audience was over, then called me back.

"I want to hear the instrument. Where do you live? I'll come to your house."

Since I lived three blocks away, this was simple, but I only half-expected to see him again.

A few days later the phone rang.

"This is Dionysis. I will come by to hear the harpsichord."

I put down the telephone feeling sick with fear. I found this man intimidating and I wasn't at all sure I could mimic what the santouri-player did. Should I prepare some food? Offer him a drink? Fortunately, I had very little time to wait.

He arrived half an hour later with a beautiful and very young guitar-player.

He asked me to play something, tapped at the keyboard himself, and after a few seconds, nodded his head.

"This is Theologos. He knows the show. He'll help you," he said. "And you'll come to the show for the next ten days until the santouri-player leaves."

I had my orders. I was in the band.

That night, when I arrived at the club, Theologos took me into what looked like a broom-closet where the musicians huddled before they played. It was so small they were literally sitting on top of each other. They were very different from Theodorakis's musicians. With their beards, jeans, and long hair they looked like any band might look in America, France, or England. They smiled and welcomed me with a minimum of fuss and went back to their laughter and talk.

That night I sat near the front of the audience, eyes and ears fixed on the santouri.

The same routine went on for a week. Each night I went to one or both shows. In the afternoon, Theologos came by and we worked on the music. At the end of the week, Savvopoulos came to see how I was doing. He sat close to the harpsichord, and pronounced this bit good, that, not what he wanted. Whatever he wanted from me he had to sing or play on his guitar. I would imitate it until it satisfied him. It was an odd way to orchestrate a piece, but I realized he had a good sense of the musical effect he was after. By the end of the hour we had a rudimentary score.

Musically, I wasn't so excited by Savvopoulos; culturally, he was the most influential performer in Greece. Theologos and the other musicians in the band interested me as much as Savvopoulos. Unlike the players in Theodorakis's band, these young players and singers were not stars. Some would become famous, but not yet. They were all good musicians and they were glad to be playing with the man who had redefined Greek music in the 1970's. They would be my companions and friends for the next two months as we played, traveled, ate, slept and recorded together. I was curious about their musical tastes and what made them turn to Savvopoulos rather than Theodorakis. I found that they listened to Pink Floyd and Bob Dylan in their spare time rather than to Greek music. They liked rembetika music, but they were tired of the politically charged music their parents had idealized. Savvopoulos was something different. He used electric guitars and rock drums; his songs were about the world they'd grown up in. Among young Greeks he was the epitome of cool.

Athens is a late city. The second show finished around 1 a.m. After that we'd go out to eat. The nearest restaurant that would serve a large group at 1.30 in the morning was in an old basement. The food and wine were generic but they never minded how late we stayed. In the warm, smoky fug of the basement, with a jug of wine in front of us, we fell on the food like the stray cats of Anafiotika. Sakis, a large singer with an operatic bass voice who sang the part of General Lamarchos, would trumpet a few lines from a song. Angelos, the bearded sound-engineer, would treat us to whole scenes from the Karaghiozis shadow-puppet theater, playing all the parts. Savvopoulos would throw a sarcastic aside to him and we would all soon be in a hilarious mood. Sometimes it was three o'clock, sometimes four, before I picked up my heavy portable harpsichord and staggered the three blocks to my apartment on the corner of Rangava Street.

Clubs like *Rigas* are only open in the winter season. In the late spring, if a show has been successful, the entertainer takes it on the road. I discovered we were booked on a tour that would take us all over Greece during the month of May. Then we would come back to Athens to make a recording of the show in a studio. We did our traveling shows only at week-ends, so we would set out on a Thursday or Friday and come back to Athens on Monday. The first week-end in May we were to play in Patras.

I've always liked the market-towns of Greece where people come from the villages to sell their goods at week-ends. They are not the most beautiful towns of Greece, but they are busy towns where villagers meet and gypsies come to play music or trade goods. Around the bus stations of the market towns are some of the cheapest and best restaurants in Greece. You can point to oily vats of green peas, eggplants, zucchini, moussaka, and pastitsio, which the owner will slop in generous dollops onto thick white plates. With a hunk of crusty bread and a glass or two of retsina to cut the oil, you can eat like a pasha.

We arrived at Patras in time for lunch and I looked forward to the joys of its simple food. I had reckoned without the fact that I was traveling with famous people. Savvopoulos, his wife, and the singer Melina Tanagra went off to eat at a fancy restaurant in the town and suggested I join them, but the boys in the band knew about a little place in the fish-market that was not to be missed, and I decided to join them. We walked off towards the port as the market was closing and found a small café right on the wharf. Patras looks over a narrow strip of sea to the Aetolia-Akarnania mountains. They rise straight out of the sea. Gods, goats and nymphs may frolic on their slopes. Nothing else could possibly climb them. We sat in warm spring sun feasting on the view, the fresh fish, and a wine that was pink, careless, and spring-like. By the time we got to the second liter we had forgotten all about the concert and were all a little in love with each other. Some of the musicians went back to the hotel to sleep it off. I walked to the end of the pier with one of the singers to dream a little longer.

That night we played better than we had ever played in Athens. The enchanted lunch seemed to last us through the evening and lingered as we headed home to Athens through the dark spring night. Angelos treated us to a scene from one of the Karaghiozis plays, and those who were weren't asleep joined in.

"Look," said the singer next to me. "Daybreak!"

We had crossed the Corinth Canal and were speeding past the flaming oil refineries of Skaramangas towards the city. The pale concrete mass of Athens rose out of the dusty suburbs, with the Acropolis stuck like a tourist postcard on a pedestal above it. We were home.

Crete, Corfu, Thessaloniki. Each week-end was heady with success. Thessaloniki is Savvopoulos's home town. The crowd was so impatient at the cinema where we were to perform that they broke down the plate glass doors to get in. After each show the wine and food and laughter lasted until morning. When the tour ended we started to record the music in a studio in Athens. It was more demanding work than the nightly shows we knew by heart. Savvopoulos changed the orchestration, making me play piano as well as harpsichord, adding instruments, ad-libbing as he went along. When we finished, the annual exodus from Athens to the islands and the countryside would begin and we would all go our separate ways. Already there was a distance between us as the days in the studio dwindled. On the day it was released, Savvopoulos's *Acharnians* sold 10,000 copies, a record number for Greece.

You can hear the album here: goo.gl/3G6NQl

17. Aristophanes at Epidaurus

The heat rose off the pavements of Athens like a hairdryer in your face and the air was thick with diesel fuel. Theodorakis was conducting the Athens Radio Orchestra, who would be performing his *First Symphony* and since I was working on the last chapters of my book about his music, he suggested I come along to rehearsals so that we could talk in the breaks. He would pick me up early in the morning on the way to Ayia Paraskevi, where the rehearsals took place, and drop me off on his way home. I waited each morning for the sound of the horn and raced downstairs before a crowd gathered to stare. Often we talked about music, but with Theodorakis, the conversation drifted in all directions – politics, gossip, memories of exile and imprisonment. One day we stopped for gas at a small garage. The owner filled the tank, and when Theodorakis tried to pay, he said, "Not for you," and waved him on. Theodorakis smiled but the man just looked at him with a serious expression.

"He was probably on Makronissos or Ikaria," Mikis said. "Who knows what his story is?

"They were savage days. When they transported prisoners to Ikaria, the boats were small and the prisoners were handcuffed. The trip before I came to the island a storm hit them not far off shore. The prisoners were afraid they'd be drowned if the boat capsized, and they asked the crew to take off their handcuffs, but they refused. Twenty-six prisoners were drowned.

"A storm hit our boat too, off Evia. It was a regular passenger boat taking people across to the island. We were handcuffed to each other in pairs. We begged them the take our handcuffs off, but they just ignored us. The worst thing was that none of the passengers took our side. They called out 'Dogs!' 'Scum!' 'You all deserve to die!'

"I was handcuffed to a very short man from Kalamata. I remember he had half an ear missing from the torture and the beatings. There was no-one on board who wasn't bleeding. We had to get up in pairs to piss over the side. There was vomit everywhere, but one of the prisoners found a guitar – God knows how – and began to play some music handcuffed to his mate. Those were the things that kept us going. They were terrible days!"

We pulled up at the security gate of the radio station. "Hi Mikis," said the guard, and the demons that haunted the composer were banished for a while.

The *First Symphony* sounded fine to me in the rehearsal but Theodorakis was not happy.

"I wonder if any of them knows or cares how this piece was written, on scraps of paper between the murders and the beatings. The symphony is all about that time, the Civil War and afterwards. I began it on Ikaria, and went on working on it in Athens and on Makronissos. All during that time I lived with the symphony. That's what kept me sane, the inspiration. The only thing these musicians think about is finishing the rehearsal and getting paid."

The Greek musicians' union was a strong one, and I was astonished to see how strictly they kept to their "work-to-rules" agreement. It didn't matter if they were in the middle of a movement; once the bassist held up his hand, it was time for a coffee break. This infuriated Mikis, but gave us plenty of time to talk.

When I went to get my coffee at the bar, the talk was about everything except music. The only time the musicians talked about the music was to say how surprised they were that Theodorakis was an excellent conductor. Most of them only knew him as a writer of popular songs.

"Not like the last one," a violinist said, referring to a well-known

Greek conductor. "It was a real mistake to look at him. Even when you watched his feet tapping it was hopeless. In the end we agreed to look at the first violin instead."

Beethoven's Sixth Symphony was the other work on the program, and the orchestra weren't playing it the way Theodorakis liked, especially the slow movement. On the second morning he said to the orchestra:

"I see this movement as mauve. Just think mauve and you'll play it better."

Suddenly, the strings began to float. I sat at the back of the sound-stage lost in a lavender sea. "Waves!" called Mikis. When they finished the musicians were all smiling.

"That's it. Mauve," he repeated, pleased with them and himself.

On the way home he spoke about his father, who had died recently.

"My father died twice," he told me. The first time, when they gave him an injection in the hospital, he thought it was the end. He called me to tell me to come because it was the end."

" 'Father,' I asked him, 'Are you pleased with your life?' And he said,

" 'How could I be anything else with a son who's made our name blessed in the whole world?'

"We were both weeping, but the next day he was fine. He died again a few days later."

I remembered the film footage of Mikis's 'trial' under the junta. His father stood beside him, white-faced, with dark circles under his eyes. How many times had he stood beside his son before and after the torture or exile, desperately pulling every string he could to try to free him from Makronissisos or another prison camp, watching him led away, or welcoming him home on crutches?

"There was a great love in our house," said Mikis. "I never saw a quarrel there. My mother died soon after my father and the last words she said were, "Yorgos, I'm coming."

"He was a vegetarian, my father. I don't mean literally. But he and my brother and my son – they're all vegetarians by nature. My daughter and I are carnivores."

One day after rehearsal, Theodorakis told me he had a surprise for me. We drove into town and parked near the winter headquarters of the Koun Theater.

The basement theater was still cool, and a group of musicians were gathered on stage rehearsing. A young man with a beard and thick-lensed glasses was directing the rehearsal. When we entered they broke off. Two of the musicians were familiar faces. I had played with them before. One had played in Savvopoulos's band with me for months.

Mikis took over the rehearsal. The music was for another Aristophanes' play, *The Knights*, in a new production by the Koun Theater. Theodorakis had been commissioned to compose the score that spring. It was interesting music, full of odd rhythms, and I could see the musicians were enjoying themselves. They were, as usual, all male. The

Music rehearsal

singers in the chorus were all male too, since there are no female characters in *The Knights*. The Koun Theatre had a permanent chorus of men and women. To give the women in the theater company enough work, they would perform Euripides' *Trojan Women*, with its female chorus and predominantly female cast, at the same festival.

When the rehearsal finished, one of the musicians called out to Theodorakis:

"Put Gail in the band. She's a good musician."

Theodorakis looked at me. "Do you like the music?"

"Yes," I said, "It sounds wonderful."

"Hmm, it's not a bad idea." Theodorakis looked at the musicians and then at me. "We could use a mare in the stable."

The musicians all burst out laughing and I had a new job.

The Koun Theatre was by far the most innovative and exciting theatre company in Greece and I was thrilled to be working with them. Karolos Koun, who founded the theatre was now an old man, and he left the most of the rehearsals to his assistant, but I knew that his style of direction still dominated the theater. Koun was the first director to stage Ionesco, Tennessee Williams, Chekov, and Brecht in Greece. Later he turned to productions of ancient Greek tragedy and comedy, transforming the way they were staged. His productions of Sophocles, Aeschylus, Euripides and Aristophanes had been a sensation in London, Munich, Paris, Zurich and Moscow a decade earlier. One of his great innovations was to train a permanent body of young actors and actresses for his choruses. He chose them himself, and many were from poor families. They earned very little, but they were wonderfully trained in every aspect of theater. Koun had studied his ancient sources, and he knew how important music and movement were to ancient theatre. His intention was to restore the central role of music and dance to the choruses of the plays. He commissioned the very best Greek playwrights, poets, artists, composers, and choreographers to produce his modern Greek texts and music, and to train his chorus. Then he performed his own magic on the stage. Odysseas Elytis once said, "When we are all forgotten, people will talk about the age of Koun." I hoped I would have a chance to see the legend himself, but I was told he was ill and unlikely to attend rehearsals.

Karolos Koun, theater director, at Epidaurus

The chorus spent their days rehearsing. In the

morning they rehearsed their singing parts with the musicians. In the afternoons, they worked with the choreographer on their dancing. As the Athens summer grew longer and hotter, the cool basement of the theatre slowly turned into an oven. I would set out from my apartment in the Plaka around 8a.m., when the streets were crowded with traffic. There was no point in taking a taxi because I could walk faster, so I walked the mile and a half to the theatre, cutting through the back streets. Somewhere I would grab a few sesame pretzels and a cup of coffee. The bearded young man who ran the rehearsals was Stamatis Kraounakis. He was a good conductor and he knew a lot about Greek music. He and I talked incessantly about music at every break and after rehearsals. When I told him I was writing a book about Theodorakis and that I wanted to translate it into Greek, he announced that he would be the translator.

"I'm the one who can do this," he said. "I know English quite well, my Greek is perfect, and I'm the only person in Athens who knows what you're trying to say about Mikis's music."

I was delighted with his proposition, and we decided to spend our afternoons translating the book together. Between the morning rehearsals and the afternoon translation sessions that lasted two or three hours, we would go to a small ouzo bar near Omonia Square, order an ouzo and some *mezedhes*, and have long, impassioned conversations about music, ancient drama, and Seferis. One lunchtime, Stamatis expounded his theory about the similarity between Seferis and Aeschylus. To my surprise, he told me that Seferis had translated some of the Oresteia before he died. Stamatis, who was already composing his own music, had set some of Seferis's poems to music and performed them for his widow. He was nothing if not ambitious.

"One day I'll be as famous as Theodorakis," he said. "Just watch me!"

I discovered that Stamatis still lived in his parents' house in an outer suburb of Athens. His parents were in the throes of a vicious divorce and his descriptions of their fights were beyond my belief. Once he invited me to spend the night at his house. He drowned out any background noise with improvised songs of the style you might hear in north-eastern Greece, and with words that had me laughing until I begged for mercy.

The rehearsals were hard work. They lasted from 9 a.m. to 1 a.m. and we had to work with young singers who found the score difficult. We also had to elaborate some of the instrumental arrangements for ourselves, since Theodorakis had had no time to fully orchestrate the score. Mikis would turn up at an occasional rehearsal, injecting new life into the score, adding a chorus here, subtracting something there, making us feel ashamed if he didn't like an arrangement we had made, talking to the boys in the chorus about politics, and clowning. When the costumes were ready for the chorus of knights, they were difficult to manage. They were horse-shaped and made of papier maché so that the wearer stepped into them, looking something like a centaur. The body and head of the construction were covered in newspapers cut and pasted on, with headlines about contemporary Greek politics. The moment he saw them, Theodorakis picked up a horse mask, put it on his head and began conducting with a giant phallus intended for the leader of the chorus.

Theodorakis clowning with horse mask

August was here and the performance was drawing near. We were to travel with the chorus to the village of Ligourion, near the ancient site of Epidaurus and live there for a week, rehearsing and performing. It is a tradition that when the Epidaurus Festival is in session, the villagers rent rooms to the performers. The village, which is not large, is packed for weeks with actors, musicians, directors, and theatre-goers. Stamatis and I were billeted in the same house.

Our landlady, Panayiotitsa, we discovered, made the best Greek coffee we had ever drunk. Our dress rehearsal was scheduled for the following night. The night we arrived it was the turn of the women. I hadn't yet seen any rehearsals of the *Trojan Women*. They were held at another theatre in downtown Athens. Now I had my first opportunity to see a full-scale Koun production. Another tradition of the Epidaurus Festival is that the people of Ligourion are given free admission to the dress rehearsals. This is not only a reward for hospitality but gives the actors a chance to perform before a live audience.

The word magical is easy to use in Greece. The landscape is peopled with ghosts, not just the ghosts of the ancients, but the ghosts of the Philhellenes who have written so much about it. Epidaurus is one of the few places in Greece where you can perfectly recapture the influence of the physical landscape on the structure that stands on it, or in this case, embraces it. The theater's acoustics are astonishing. Epidauris is built *because* of its physical setting, not in spite of it. A whisper center-stage can be heard in the highest row of stone seats. There is something more, here, than the natural amphitheater amplifying sound, something harder to grasp. The light was fading as we entered the theatre and a summer smell of pines and dust filled the air. The villagers talked idly as they waited. Stamatis, who would be playing percussion in the performance, searched his bag frantically for a drum. There was not much in the way of scenery, just burned-out timber barrels spread out on the circular marble stage. When the actors entered, in their ragged grey costumes, they too looked burned, as if they had been charred in a fire.

The first stars were out. The beautiful young girl who played Cassandra made her entrance from the ramped hillside under the pines, her dress a flutter of yellow, a flaming torch in each hand, singing as she walked. Stamatis was still hunting for his drum:

"Clap!" he whispered. I stood at the back of the stage, clapping the rhythm as the chorus sang. There were no other musicians for this performance, and I was terrified I'd make a mistake. Stamatis, I said to myself, hurry! I looked up at the curved rows of marble steps thinly sprinkled with villagers, and I tried to imagine how it could ever have filled in ancient times. The theater holds fifteen thousand people. How did they travel? Where did they come from? How many would come to hear us on Saturday night? The drum found, Stamatis took over, and I was free to turn my attention to the play.

The saddest of Euripides' plays is all about women: Hecuba, Andromache, Cassandra, Helen. Among the charred ruins and smoky costumes, Helen's costume glowed deep pink like a flame. Her face was as white as a kabuki puppet's. An actress I'd seen gossiping and laughing in the village had been transformed, as Hecuba, into an ancient crone. I wanted to concentrate on Euripides' words, but I was too overwhelmed by the experience of being here. I couldn't stop staring around me at the theater, the sky turning navy blue, the moon rising behind the pines. In a few nights I would be performing here. We were the first musicians to play in a production of ancient drama since antiquity. Before this, modern revivals had been performed with a pre-recorded score. Two small stages were built specially for us so that three musicians could play on either side of the stage. Tears came to my eyes, not for Hecuba's agony, but for the wonder of this theater and my being a small part of it.

Like all performances of ancient drama in Greece, the play was translated into colloquial Greek. Very soon after the foundation of the modern Greek state, tragedies and comedies had been translated into Greek. The rhetoric of the plays, particularly of Aristophanes' comedies, was irresistible as a vehicle to satirize modern Greek political life. It was also a literary challenge to preserve not only the scurrilous humor of the original texts, but the beauty of Aristophanes' verse. Some of Greece's leading playwrights were commissioned to produce modern versions of the dramas and comedies, making them accessible to an audience as broad as the one that must have filled the theater of Dionysos in Athens.

When the rehearsal ended, the people of Ligourion all sat silent for a moment, stunned by Euripides' tragedy, and by the performance. Then they burst into loud applause. I realized they were an excellent audience partly because they had so many productions to compare this to.

While her husband worked outside in the searing afternoon sun, staking tomatoes, Panayiotitsa would break a handful of small, bitter almonds for me with a stone. Green lizards flicked in and out the gaps in the stones. The garden gave off a smell of dust and ripeness. We sat in companionable silence, chewing almonds.

That night it began to rain softly. I listened to the drops falling on the vines outside my window and fell into a deep sleep. In the morning the air was heavy and the temperature had dropped twenty degrees. We were glad of the coolness, but there was rising tension about the possibility of rain during the performance. In the evening we set out for the first rehearsal in the theatre, all of us nervous, including Theodorakis.

We had been rehearsing with the chorus, not the principal actors, and we had no idea of how the play looked as a whole. We had also never seen some of the chorus members dancing on stilts. One of Koun's strokes of genius was to substitute stilts for the second level of the *skiniko*, the fixed

The chorus of The Knights dancing

set at the back of the stage. During the ancient performances, gods made their appearances from openings high above the stage, creating the effect of a *deus ex machina*, that must have thrilled the audience. With the *skiniko* of Epidaurus destroyed, the effect was lost. Koun had used stilts famously for his production of *Peace*, and they were such a success that he would use them again for the finale of *The Knights*. If the stage was even slightly wet, the stilts would slip on the stone and hard earth stage.

Theodorakis had hired a classical flute-player to perform with us. He was a serious young musician and Mikis had written out a part for him. Stamatis had been rehearsing it on a recorder, and none of us had met the flutist before. He sat down next to me and said, without irony, "I don't know what it is about this place, but I feel physically well sitting here."

I wondered if he knew anything about Asklepius, or the fact that this was the most famous healing center of the classical world. In antiquity, and even well into the Christian period, visitors traveled from far away to the sanctuary of Apollo's son Asklepius, the great healer. They would spend the night in the *enkoimitiria*, a large dormitory where the god would advise them, in their dreams, about what they should do to regain their health. If it hadn't been for the money that the grateful patients brought to the sanctuary, the theater could never have been built. Ancient sites weren't chosen for nothing. Perhaps there was something about this small corner of the Peloponnese that promoted a feeling of well-being.

Despite its location, the rehearsal went badly. The lead actor was supposed to enter on a see-saw, but when a member of the chorus tested it, it broke. The chorus, separated from the musicians, and without Stamatis beside them, sang out of tune. We only had one more rehearsal before the performance, and Mikis was worried about the length of some of the choruses. The cool change had affected my harpsichord which was almost a semitone sharp. There were objections from the other musicians and I promised to tune it down for the following night.

The music was not easy, and during the rehearsals, Stamatis, whose ambition was to be the new Hadzidakis and Theodorakis combined, realized how cleverly Theodorakis had set each word, each line of the chorus. He intended, he said, to steal every trick he could from the master when he composed his own music. We were both sad when Mikis decided to make large cuts in the score, but we realized that the production needed tightening. Everything seemed off kilter that night. After a tense evening meal, there was a fight between some of the actors and a group of local boys over a dance, and we all went to bed in low spirits.

The next day we decided to escape from the village and we drove to Nafplion for lunch. The food at the restaurant we chose was bad but the wine was good. We all began to sing, and the mood of the actors began to improve. On the way back to the village we picked up two young Viennese tourists who seemed amazed by our hilarity. We only had a short time to rest before the rehearsal, but with the wine still in my head I dozed, dreaming a healing dream in which yellow, orange and pink clouds floated above me. When I woke I had no time to enjoy Panayiotitsa's coffee; it was time to tune the harpsichord down to A440. By the time the other musicians arrived, the flute-player and I were in perfect tune, but Andreas, the third musician on our platform, was having trouble with his tuba. There was nothing I could do about it, so I went to the low stone building where the dressing-rooms were and found I had one to myself. It even had my name on the door. For the dress rehearsal, we were told, we would wear costumes. Nobody had mentioned this before, and no measurements had been taken. I wondered what we would be required to wear, and hoped, rather foolishly, that it would be flattering. In the dressing-room, on the back of my chair, was a loose cotton tunic in a deep shade of terracotta. Beside the mirror was a wreath made of olive branches, with ribbons hanging from it in terracotta and green. It looked splendid, but was stiff and prickly to wear. I looked in the mirror. In my new clothes I felt like a star, a smudge of light in the Greek sky.

This time the rehearsal went well. An old man was helped into the stalls at the beginning of the performance. Someone in the chorus pointed him out to me and said "Koun!" I tried to keep him in the corner of my eye as I played, waiting to see his reaction. His assistant sat next to him and Koun pointed to the stage several times. I knew he would be doing what he was famous for: making the last minute changes that would lift the production into another sphere. One of the actors told me that years earlier when they had performed Aeschylus here, the chorus didn't have the intonation he wanted when they called on the chthonic spirits. Koun made them kneel on the ground and eat some dirt. "If you want to understand the spirits of the lower earth, you have to eat earth!" he shouted.

As the rehearsal ended and the villagers continued to cackle at Aristophanes' bawdy jokes, rain sprinkled the stage. We were all nervous for the week-end's performances. Rain would ruin everything, and there would be no chance of re-scheduling. We held our breath and went to sleep earlier than usual.

On Friday night the rain began — not just a sprinkle, this time, but a downpour. By midday the sky cleared, but what would the theater be like? We drove out to see whether there had been any damage and found a scene that could hardly have been more depressing. The electricians and stage-hands were standing beside the stage, which was ankle-deep in water. A decision had to be made soon whether to cancel the performance. Even if the sun stayed out, the actors realized, the stage would be a sea of mud and there was no way they could use stilts. While we stood miserably beside the stage, Theodorakis's son Yorgos, who played percussion with the tympanum-player, said he remembered reading somewhere that there was a stone in the middle of the stage that was used, in ancient times, to drain the water off. This sounded an unlikely story, and the thought of a stone plug still being in place was fantastic, but Yorgos rolled up his pants and began to wade towards the middle of the stage. We laughed, despite our misery, and watched him for fifteen minutes as he lifted one long skinny leg up after another like a heron, feeling for the stone.

Then the impossible happened. He announced he had found a large stone right there in the middle of the stage, and the technicians waded into the water to join him. They lifted up the stone as we all shouted encouragement. To everyone's disbelief, the water slowly began to drain toward the centre of the stage. We whooped and laughed, throwing our arms around Yorgos as we watched the muddy soil appear, but even when there was no more water left lying on the circle of earth, the actors realized that the stage would be impossible to dance on. The director and some more of the company had arrived and the general consensus was that the performance would have to be cancelled; dancing and walking on stilts on a stage slippery with mud would simply be too dangerous. A conversation began among the stage hands that I missed and a car set off for the village. We followed, wondering if we had missed our chance to perform in what must be the most spectacular theater in the world. While we were eating lunch a message arrived. Someone had ordered a load of hay from a local farmer and they were busy spreading it all over the stage. Hay and horsemen — what could be more appropriate for Aristophanes' comedy? The set would look like a stable. If the rain held off, we might have our performance.

That afternoon we all watched the sky. Clouds still hung in pillowy masses over the mountains but they cleared as evening approached. We set out for the theater, nervous and excited. For me, this would be a chance to vindicate myself as a musician. Last time I played for Theodorakis in public the band was loud, the harpsichord was always out of tune by the end of a performance, and I felt a failure. This time we had rehearsed for months. I knew my part, and I was confident that the harpsichord would hold its tune.

When we reached the theater, tour buses were already lined up in the parking lot. I recognized some of the people sitting in the theatre café. Mikis was sitting with a group of people who had the confident look of the famous. Stamatis pointed out writers, actresses, film-directors, even the poet Odysseas Elytis. I knew that Theodorakis was nervous too, but he was joking and laughing with his friends as if he hadn't a care. I realized that he had no function at this performance. He would sit with his friends in the audience looking relaxed and praying that the music sounded as he intended. Suddenly I was terrified. There were so few of us - just six musicians in a theatre that would be filled with as many as fifteen thousand people. What if one of us lost their place?

In the stone dressing-room I changed into my costume. I fantasized that it was the room Maria Callas used when she performed her legendary *Medea* here, but she probably had at least three rooms to herself. I was happy to be wearing my terracotta robe with the crown of olives that half-hid my face. The color of the costume was flattering and I decided to look for a dress in just this shade when I got back to Athens, somewhere between tomato and brick. I noticed my hands were beginning to shake.

The booming voice of Katerina interrupted my attack of nerves. She had come by boat and bus from Aigina. I was surprised and delighted she had come, but unable to give her my full attention. Katerina, of course, knew who all the famous people were and would give me a rundown, later, on the love life of Athenians in the audience. The chorus was nervous of dancing, especially on stilts, in the hay. This was a completely different surface to the one they had rehearsed on. What if they slipped? It was too late to test the surface now. We had our last sound check and I decided the harpsichord was in good tune. The only person who seemed to have no nerves at all was the flute player. The theatre itself was performing its magic, keeping him in a state of well-being. Stamatis was the one who must hold the musicians and chorus together. He told us all we would be sensational, but I could see beads of sweat on his forehead. A lot was hanging on this performance for him too.

As we took our seats on the small raised platforms I looked up at the full theatre. There was still an apricot glow in the sky above the pines, but the first stars were out. Thousands of Greeks and tourists were seated in the stone amphitheatre and the late-comers were making their way to their seats. It must always have been so. Visitors from all parts of Greece and even from across the water in Asia Minor came here more than two thousand years ago to see performances of tragedy and comedy. Some must have traveled for weeks to reach the theatre and been stunned by its size and beauty, by the perfection of its acoustics. Stamatis, wearing his own robe and crown, gave us a wicked smile and whacked the drum with a big stick. The show had begun.

I can't remember much about the performance. All I know is that nothing disastrous occurred. Koun's last-minute changes and Mikis's cuts had improved the production. The newspaper-covered horses galloped safely on the straw, the stilt-walkers did not fall. The chorus sang in tune, the musicians stayed together. At the end of the performance we were all dizzy with relief and excitement, but I was overcome with longing to stay here in this enchanted space for another night, another week. I had hardly understood what happened here tonight. Another performance and I would be able to concentrate on the music, the acoustics, the play itself. Instead the musicians were packing up their instruments for the night, and tomorrow we would return to Athens. The sound engineer passed me on the way out.

"The harpsichord sounded great tonight," he said. "I'll make you a copy of the recording."

We drove back to the village talking incessantly, as all performers do, about the details of the performance. Katerina had come specially to see me, but we were soon caught up with the euphoric chatter of a successful show. This was my night, my last glorious night in Epidaurus and I joined in the mad ecstasy of the table of actors and musicians. Mikis was far away with his family and friends. I waited for his nod of approval but I no longer needed it. The moon still hung in the summer sky, the wine flowed, and soon we would dance.

When we reached Athens the next day we heard that the sound technician, who drove his truck back to Athens after the performance, had fallen asleep at the wheel. His truck ran off the road and he was killed instantly. I never did hear the recording of my only performance in the theatre with the best acoustics in the world.

Gods

In the flicker of oil-lamps
their shadows are tall as cypresses.
We made them simulacra of ourselves,
tall enough to frighten or impress.
Imagine a world without them —
who would fight far
from home or sacrifice his child?
And if their clay feet
protrude beneath their robes,
try not to look down
but up at their onyx eyes.

Spider Woman

For Diamanda Galas

She may have lost to a goddess but she won
in the end. The goddess long dead,
Arachne still wove and spun
until she'd made a steely thread

strong enough to catch a wasp.
See, she whispers to each creature
struggling to escape the sure grasp
of her web, *this is my revenge. Nature*

has remedies for a curse. I honed my skill,
enduring while the gods died fighting
disbelief. A plain weaver still,
I watch you die and wrap a winding

sheet of white silk tight
around you. Athena made me monstrous
but left my skill intact: an oversight.
Art outlasts the gods that curse us.

Buried Treasure

Water old as dinosaurs
lies under the Greek earth.
Dig a well and it fills
with clear fossil water
or did until yesterday.
Now no-one drinks

the water of Argos; a thousand
wells have drained the plain
where Agamemnon's horses grazed.
Tankers bring liquid treasure
to the Aegean islands in summer
so sweating tourists can bathe.

They don't ask where
this treasure comes from;
content to feel its coolness
on their skin they stand,
eyes closed like Danäe
in her shower of liquid gold.

Lemons

Take the lemon from a Matisse
and all the light is gone.
Oranges offer nothing
to the painter but colored balls.
The lemon's warty rind
sweats like human skin.

A boy selling lemons
in the Cairo traffic transports
an Egyptian poet to his village.
Slices of lemon remind
Ritsos that death's cart
may come with yellow wheels.

In the movie *Atlantic City*
Susan Sarandon rubs
wedges of lemon on her breasts
to smother the smell of fish
while a man at a window follows
its path across warm skin.

A man I knew was cutting
lemons and left the knife lying
on the sink. When he came home
he found his girl dead,
stabbed in fourteen places
by the knife he'd used

to cut lemons for a soufflé.
Who picked up the knife
or drove its whetted edge
into her they never discovered.
Afterwards he made me soufflés
from the lemons on his tree.

At Epidaurus One Night.

In memoriam Karolus Koun

If you want to understand the chthonic gods
eat dirt, the director said
and the chorus got down on their knees
to taste a mouthful of earth at Epidaurus.

He took Aristophanes' *Birds* to Berlin,
Oedipus to London, but this giant horseshoe,
ancient hearth of healing and drama,
was where he felt most at home.

When I saw him he was old and ugly
as Socrates. His protégé held him upright
till they reached the lowest tier of seats
where judges sat in another age.

After each scene he made his critique
filtered through an assistant's mask
—his voice had lost its power to carry
even in that acoustic paradigm.

The actors listened,
a taste of earth in their mouths.

18. Once in a Lifetime

When I visited Mariza in 2007, my first book of poetry, *Penelope's Confession*, had just come out in English and Greek. Mariza had no sooner received the poems than she began setting some of them to music. It had been the hottest summer on record in Greece, and after years of drought, the country caught fire. First the fires burned around Athens and on the islands, then they broke out in the Peloponnese. By the end of September half of the forests of southern Greece had been destroyed and sixty-five people had died. Mariza was in Kardamyli, on the coast of the Peloponnese and she saw the fires raging above the town. I called her on her cell phone to see if she was safe, and she said she'd had to hide in the house because she couldn't stop crying.

"Elektra, I had to stop working on your poems. I couldn't do anything except weep. I went down to the sea to get cool, but the water was full of ash, greasy black flakes. But you'll have a book-launching – I've arranged it at the most *in* place in Athens. And I'll sing the two songs I've finished."

It was a crazy time to launch a book in Greece — first the fires, then a national election, with the government struggling to persuade everyone that the fires were the result of a conspiracy by Greece's enemies and that their response to the fires was adequate, and the Opposition blaming the government for everything. What was worse I had come to Greece on a working trip and had only three days in Athens. I realized that I was expected to find people to present the book.

I could count on my brilliant Katerina, I knew, to read the poems, some of which she had translated, in Greek, but who should introduce me? I dreamt of asking Theodorakis, but that was impossible – he hardly went anywhere any more, even to performances of his own music.

Then it occurred to me that Iakovos Kambanellis might be prepared to do it. Despite his eighty-three years he still supervised rehearsals of his plays, and we had a very special relationship that began with my translation of *Mauthausen* and continued over my visits to Athens. We almost always managed to sit for a couple of hours together in a café and talk about his latest play, or a poem I had written. I called him before I left and asked him rather nervously if he might present the book, perhaps together with Katerina.

"Of course I will," he answered, sounding buoyant as a man of fifty. "It will be a pleasure."

He called me at Mariza's house the day before the reading. We were playing with the latest in a string of pets that dominated her household, a tabby kitten called Liveloula (Dragonfly) with ears as long her ancient Egyptian ancestors.

"You know," said Kambanellis, "I've been talking to Katerina and we decided not to do the usual thing that goes on here at book-launchings, with these silly flattering speeches. What people want to hear is why you wrote the poems in Greek as well as English. That's an interesting story, and what we'll do is interview you so that people can understand who you are."

As a man of the theater, Kambanellis wanted dialogue and drama, not speeches.

Mariza had invited a young musician to accompany her as she sang the song-setting of the poems. He was a boy from Santorini who played the oud.

"He sings so well – a real Byzantine voice! I might let him perform the first song. See what you think."

The young man who arrived to rehearse the songs not only had a

Byzantine voice, he looked like an icon, with a thin line of black beard framing his oval face.

Mariza had made my poems her own, cutting out what she didn't want, rearranging lines, but she had turned them into lovely songs. The words I had written were now music, Mariza's music… *Ifadhi ble, stimoni ble* – weft blue, warp blue –it sounded so lovely sung in Greek. I still found it hard to believe that after so many years of translating Greek words and music into English, I was being translated into Greek song.

That night Mariza had a dream. She saw all of Athens destroyed by an earthquake. In her dream she turned on the TV and a reporter announced cheerfully that fortunately, only 1,500 people had been killed.

"I don't think it was a prophetic dream, Elektra. The night before Yorgos (her brother-in-law) died, I saw a man in a frock coat. He wasn't wearing any pants. He was walking towards a woman who was trying to get away from him. When I see a naked man, that's the only time I know for certain something bad is going to happen."

We arrived early at the bookstore and the only people there were the musician and a technician setting up the microphones. I was afraid no-one would come and it would be fiasco. A minute later Kambanellis arrived looking elegant but frail, and gave me his usual boyish smile. "Don't worry," he said. Katerina and I will ask the questions. All you have to do is answer."

Katerina's entrances were never quiet. "Gailaki!" she shouted, using the diminutive of my name as usual and turning all heads in her direction. Her English was superb, and she would never have resorted to a Greek name for me. Still, she couldn't resist the Greek ending. Her hair, cut like a twenties flapper, had been restored to its original black with a reddish tinge to it, and her lips were scarlet. I liked the bold new look. She was always at her best when she had to perform.

The event passed like a dream you can't quite recall at dawn. The high points were Mariza's singing, Katerina's bravura reading of her Greek translations of the poems, Kambanellis's theatrical flair as an interviewer, and the unexpected arrival of Theodorakis, who appeared like a *deus ex machina* from a small service elevator I hadn't noticed in the shop. He sat to one side because he didn't want to be seen being helped to walk. Once seated, he looked his old self.

I can't remember a word of what I said. At some point I looked around and realized how many of the people in the room were old, people I had idolized all my life, people who belonged to 'That Generation.' Mikis Theodorakis, Iakovos Kambanellis, Katerina Anghelaki-Rooke, the film director Nikos Koundouros. And Mariza. They had come for my little book of poems. I couldn't help the tears. And when I looked through them, everyone looked young again.

"Mariza, sing the songs again," I begged when the reading was over. I couldn't bear the moment to end. The oud player joined her and the sound filled the bookstore. Their voices blended like singers in an Orthodox Church service on the island they both came from, Santorini. I watched the one face I trusted to judge the music. Theodorakis was smiling quietly.

"Elektra," Mariza said when we went back to her apartment. "Remember this. You'll never be able to do it again. That's the sort of thing you do once in your lifetime."

Epilogue

Che fece...il gran rifiuto

Σε μερικούς ανθρώπους έρχεται μια μέρα
που πρέπει το μεγάλο Ναι ή το μεγάλο Όχι
να πούνε. Φανερώνεται αμέσως όποιος τ᾽οχει
έτοιμο μέσα του το Ναι, και λέγοντάς το πέρα

πηγαίνει στην τιμή και στην πεποίθησή του.
Ο αρνηθείς δεν μετανοιώνει. Αν ρωτιούνταν πάλι,
όχι θα ξαναέλεγε. Κι όμως τον καταβάλλει
εκείνο τ᾽όχι –το σωστό—εις όλην την ζωή του.

Che fece...il gran rifiuto

For certain people there comes a day
to utter the great Yes or the great No.
Whoever it is will quickly show
he has the yes in him ready to say;

And with conviction and honor, on he'll go.
The no-sayer never repents what he denied;
he would say no again if he were tried.
Yet his life is weighed down by that proper no.

C.P. Cavafy (my translation)

"This continual concern for the aliens must come to an end once and for all... I could not care less when you say that people under your administration are dying of hunger. Let them perish so long as no German starves."

–Hermann Göring. Letter to the Reich commissioners and military commanders of the occupied territories. August 6, 1942.

In a season of steadily worsening depression, July 2015 will be remembered as a month of extraordinary drama. Occupying the center of the world stage for months, Greece gambled against its creditors and lost. For a day, the word NO thundered in the streets again, as it had done when General Metaxas said no to the Italians, and the historical echo gave most Greeks a renewed sense of national pride. It was bound to be brief; the Greeks held no cards in their hands and the majority of its citizens wanted to stay in the Euro-zone, but neither did they have any hope of defeating the German military machine in 1940 as it rescued the Italians from the attacking Greek army and occupied Greece. In both cases their 'no' cost the Greeks dearly. And probably many of them would say no again.

On July 29th, Mikis Theodorakis turned 90. Manolis Glezos, who tore the Nazi flag down from the acropolis as a teenager, would be 93 in September. Their no's weighed them down for life. Torture, imprisonment, death sentences, exile — they lived their lives with a sense that the struggle mattered more than life itself. They are still struggling against the austerity measures imposed by their creditors that they see as a new form of foreign interference and domination of their country. They are extremists, leftists on the left of Syriza, but for both men, the experience of the German Occupation of their country made them what they are.

The ruination of Nazi-occupied Greece was achieved with admirable efficiency. A day after the Germans occupied Athens, Laid Archer, an American aid worker, wrote in his journal "the wholesale looting of Athens has begun." They began with food. The markets were sealed, the livestock on farms was machine-gunned. Dairy herds were confiscated. Then came transport. Cars, buses, trucks even bicycles. The contents of all shops were "bought" with worthless "Occupation Marks." Then came hospital supplies and pharmacies. As Archer wrote, "The incredible speed and efficiency of this leaves us dazed, not knowing where to turn for the most ordinary supplies."*

At the same time as they starved the Greek people, the Germans were busy photographing, preserving and excavating ancient Greek ruins, which they regarded as their own heritage. "If I had 1.5 million Reichsmarks to fund my work," their chief archeologist wrote excitedly, "the uncontested hegemony of Germany in the study of Greek monuments would be secured ... It would be so grand a gesture by the conqueror, who would show himself conscious of his cultural calling in Europe." The idea that the "cultural calling" of Germany was to lead Europe in its knowledge of ancient Greece goes back to the late eighteenth century when Johann Joachim Winkler published his *History of Art in Antiquity*. His passionate belief in the superiority of ancient Greek art over any other encouraged his fellow countrymen in the worship of all things Greek. The study of "The Classics" began in Germany and soon spread to England and France, but the Germans carried their love affair with Greece to extraordinary lengths.

In 1935, the brilliant British scholar E. M. Butler published a study of Germany's fascination with Greece entitled *The Tyran-*

ny of Greece over Germany. She concluded that among others, Goethe, Schiller, Hölderlin and Heine had carried this passion to unhealthy excess: "They wish to seize and possess Greek beauty and make it all their own; or to outdo it; or, failing that, to destroy; or to drag it violently into the present; to unearth the buried treasure; to resuscitate the gods." It was Butler who realized that Nazi ideology was intimately connected to beliefs about the superiority of ancient Greek culture. Unsurprisingly her book was banned by the Nazis.

Unlike the British philhellenes, many of whom traveled to Greece to walk on the 'hallowed ground' that had sustained its ancient inhabitants, the Germans who idealized Greece never visited the country. The ground on which the monuments stood was of no interest to them. Ancient Greece was an ideal, a foundation on which a new Germany could be built.

In Butler's view only Nietzsche understood Greece in its Dionysian, tragic form. His views were based on ancient literature, but at least he seemed to read it without blinkers. The influence of his thinking on modern Greek literature is a curious phenomenon that lasted well into the 20th century. Born on the island of Crete, educated in Germany, Nikos Kazantzakis was under Nietzsche's spell when he wrote a book that became a cliché of what modern Greece was about. The film version of *Zorba the Greek* made him an international cult figure. His Nietzschian vision of Greece turned the country into a new sort of ideal, a place where the intellectuals learn the true meaning of life from the earthy Greeks. People traveled to Greece to swim naked or nearly naked in the blue Aegean, to write novels, to smash plates at the feet of dancers. Greece, the myths suggested, was where to go to discover your Dionysian soul. A week on a Greek island, and somber Germans and British workers would be transformed. Another 1960's film,

Never on Sunday, made by the American director Jules Dassin, encouraged a similar view of Greece as a place where northerners could discard their inhibitions, if only on holiday.

Greeks have been as happy as foreigners to swallow the myth of a hedonist Greek paradise as foreigners. They may work long hours, sacrifice to educate their children, and suffer from depression, but they are happy to turn into Zorba for a night to entertain the visitors from Sweden or Germany. Their Dionysian moment in Syntagma Square after they voted "No" to the austerity measure demanded by Germany and their European creditors, was such a moment. For that moment nothing mattered but thumbing their noses at the German chancellor and her finance minister. For those on the Left and Right of Greek politics — their big "No" was the right no. Those in the middle were more cautious, and suspected there would be a price to pay.

Greeks are accustomed to seeing themselves in a mirror held up to them by philhellenes. In that mirror they have always appeared as the inferior occupiers of a land once inhabited by giants. The Great Expectations of philhellenes have cost them a great deal. Their country has been desirable and misunderstood, constantly interfered with, aided, invaded, starved and occupied. Their leaders have often been ruthless and corrupt. They have been forced to migrate to survive. And yet they have created a culture rich in literature, music, and theater, a culture of everyday living that is the envy of northern Europeans or Americans. They muddle along because they know how to take a moment – a sunset, a cup of coffee drunk in the village square, a song sung by a butcher as he chops a piece of meat, a dance on a concrete floor – and savor it. When they are least European, they understand their Greekness to be, after all, something worth having, something that will endure.

It is not a native of Greece, but a diaspora Greek who seems to have understood what Greekness means better than any other. He wrote in a cosmopolitan city, a city that had seen great days, but was shabby and well past its prime. He loved history, the history of Greeks who were not the usual figures of philhellenic imagination, but, like him, displaced from the center, exiled to colonies and outposts of the Hellenic world, Greeks who retained their Greekness through a culture and a language that remained the envy of other civilizations long after its classical moment had faded.

A brilliant man, he worked in the civil service, but never rose high in its ranks. He wrote poetry admired by some of the greatest figures of modern literature, but published no volumes in his lifetime. He was a homosexual who wrote frankly about his affairs long before it was acceptable to do so, or perhaps we could say, looking back to the poems of the Greek Anthology, long after. The decline of great societies and the minor figures of history interested him especially. He was a hedonist who admired Spartan values more than Athenian, an aesthete who preferred artificial flowers to real ones. His poems are as relevant to the Athens of today as they were to the Alexandria of his own. They are, in a time of general gloom, a comfort. Greeks, he reminds us, have always had a way of muddling through. Efforts to improve them, bring them into line, reform them, are generally futile. They will muddle through, as they have always done, because they like being as they are. It is almost a hundred years since Cavafy wrote his poem "In a Large Greek Colony, 200 BC". He wrote it about a period that interested him, a period when, in the usual view of ancient Greece, the culture, specifically of Athens, had passed its peak, and when the Roman Empire began to take an interest in the rich colonies the Greeks had established. History tells us these colonies were doomed. But Cavafy tells us something else. The reformers have no relationship with the locals, who are glad to see them leave, and will not, we imagine, take their advice too seriously.

This poem about Greeks and their reaction to austerity is as relevant today as it was then.

Ἐν Μεγάλῃ Ἑλληνικῇ Ἀποικίᾳ, 200 π.Χ.

Κωνσταντίνος Καβάφης

Ὅτι τὰ πράγματα δὲν βαίνουν κατ' εὐχὴν στὴν Ἀποικία
δέν μέν' ἡ ἐλαχίστη ἀμφιβολία,
καὶ μ' ὅλο ποὺ ὁπωσοῦν τραβοῦμ' ἐμπρός,
ἴσως, καθὼς νομίζουν οὐκ ὀλίγοι, νὰ ἔφθασε ὁ καιρός
νὰ φέρουμε Πολιτικὸ Ἀναμορφωτή.

Ὅμως τὸ πρόσκομμα κ' ἡ δυσκολία
εἶναι ποὺ κάμνουνε μιὰ ἱστορία
μεγάλη κάθε πρᾶγμα οἱ Ἀναμορφωταὶ
αὐτοί. (Εὐτύχημα θὰ ἦταν ἂν ποτέ
δέν τούς χρειάζονταν κανείς.) Γιὰ κάθε τί,
γιὰ τὸ παραμικρὸ ρωτοῦνε κ' ἐξετάζουν,
κ' εὐθὺς στὸν νοῦ τους ριζικὲς μεταρρυθμίσεις βάζουν,
μέ τὴν ἀπαίτησι νὰ ἐκτελεσθοῦν ἄνευ ἀναβολῆς.

Ἔχουνε καὶ μιὰ κλίσι στὲς θυσίες.
Παραιτηθεῖτε ἀπὸ τὴν κτῆσιν σας ἐκείνη·
ἡ κατοχή σας εἶν' ἐπισφαλής:
ἡ τέτοιες κτήσεις ἀκριβῶς βλάπτουν τὲς Ἀποικίες.
Παραιτηθεῖτε ἀπὸ τὴν πρόσοδον αὐτή,
κι ἀπὸ τὴν ἄλληνα τὴν συναφῆ,
κι ἀπὸ τὴν τρίτη τούτην: ὡς συνέπεια φυσική·
εἶναι μὲν οὐσιώδεις, ἀλλὰ τί νὰ γίνει;
σας δημιουργοῦν μιὰ ἐπιβλαβὴ εὐθύνη.

Κι ὅσο στὸν ἔλεγχό τους προχωροῦνε,
βρίσκουν καὶ βρίσκουν περιττά, καὶ νὰ παυθοῦν ζητοῦνε·
πράγματα ποὺ ὅμως δύσκολα τὰ καταργεῖ κανείς.

In a Large Greek Colony, 200 B.C.
C.P. Cavafy (my translation)

That things aren't, as one wished, working out
in the Colony there's not a shadow of a doubt.
And despite the fact we seem to be muddling along
perhaps it's time, as quite a few believe, to bring in a strong
sort of Political Reformer.

But the objections and the difficulty
is that these Reformers of society
make such a big deal out of everything
(it'd be a blessing if one never needed anything
from them). For any old thing,
the smallest detail, they start questioning
and examining, then coming
up with radical changes that they
demand be made without delay.

They have an inclination towards sacrifice:
Abandon that control;
your occupation of it is uncertain;
colonies are harmed by such a possession
Give up some of that revenue,
and the other benefits that accrue
as a natural consequence, from this third one too.
They're quite basic of course, but what to do?
They create a damaging liability for you.

And as they increase their control over the colony
they keep finding excesses to trim, things
difficult to give up in the name of austerity.

Κι ὅταν, μέ τό καλό, τελειώσουνε τήν ἐργασία,
κι ὁρίσαντες καί περικόψαντες τό πᾶν λεπτομερῶς,
ἀπέλθουν, παίρνοντας καί τήν δικαία μισθοδοσία,
νά δοῦμε τί ἀπομένει πιά, μετά
τόση δεινότητα χειρουργική. –

Ἴσως δέν ἔφθασεν ἀκόμη ὁ καιρός.
Να μή βιαζόμεθα· εἶν' ἐπικίνδυνον πρᾶγμα ἡ βία.
Τά πρόωρα μέτρα φέρνουν μεταμέλεια.
Ἔχει ἄτοπα πολλά, βεβαίως καί δυστυχῶς, ἡ Ἀποικία.
Ὅμως υπάρχει τί τό ἀνθρώπινον χωρίς ἀτέλεια;
Καί τέλος πάντων, νά, τραβούμ' ἐμπρός.

[1928]

But with any luck, when they finish their work,
arranging and pruning every little thing
they'll leave, taking their rightful perks.
We'll see what's left after
so much surgical skill –

Perhaps the time hasn't come, too.
Don't be in a hurry. A dangerous thing, haste.
We often regret a hasty course.
Certainly the colony has a host
of irregularities, to its cost,
but is there anything human without remorse?
And after all, look, we're muddling through.

Sources, further reading and listening.

I owe a great deal of information to sources in Greek, English, and French. Among the many sources I read for the war years and the German Occupation were, Roger Milliex, *Ημερολόγιο και μαρτυρίες του πολέμου και της κατοχής*, (1979), A. Marcantonatos, *A Athènes pendant la guerre: journal d'un temoin (octobre 1940 – avril 1941)*, (1976), Mark Mazower, *Inside Hitler's Greece: The Experience of Occupation 1941-1944*, (1993), Ioanna Tsatsou, *Φύλλα κατοχής* (1987), Michael Matsas, *The Illusion of Safety:The Story of the Greek Jews During the War* (1997), Marc D. Angel, *The Jews of Rhodes: The History of a Sephardic Community* (1980), Rae Dalven, *The Jews of Ioannina* 1990, Mikis Theodorakis, *Οι δρόμοι του Αρχάγελλου, 1-5*, (1986-95).

Most of my information about Theodorakis's life comes from the man himself and the many hours of conversation I have shared with him over more than forty years and which continue to this day. I am very grateful to him for his generosity and friendship. His own autobiography, *The Ways of the Archangel*, five volumes of which were published in Greek between 1986 and 1995 and which is still incomplete, has provided more details. His two volume collection of journals, poems and song texts, *To Χρέος*, published in Greek on his return to Athens in 1974, was another useful source. My own book on the man and his music: *Theodorakis: Myth and Politics in Modern Greek Music*,(1980) and translated into Greek the same year has recently been republished by Metronomos (2015) with supplementary material on later works. Guy Wager's *Mikis Theodorakis: une vie pour la Grèce*, also available in Greek, is a useful source. An invaluable source for Theodorakis's musical discography, song-texts, musical and other writings are the volumes produced by Asteris Koutoulas. The three-volume set *Μελοποιημένη ποίηση* (1997, 1999, 2001) contains the texts of all Theodorakis's compositions with brief notes. Other volumes are compilations of his musical writings and posters. Theodorakis himself is a prolific writer as well as composer and an exhaustive list of his publications would fill a book.

Katerina Anghelaki-Rooke's poetry has been translated into many languages. English editions of her books include *The Body is the Victory and the Defeat of Dreams*, (Wire Press, 1975), *Beings and Things on their Own*, (Boa, 1986), *From Purple into Night* (Shoestring, 1997) *Translating into Love Life's End* (Shoestring, 2004). A collection of translations of her poetry into English by various translators, *The Scattered Papers of Penelope*, was edited and complied by Karen Van Dyck and published by Anvil Press (2008) and Graywolf, (2009).

My translations of Nikos Kavadias's poetry are available in a dual language edition *Collected Poems of Nikos Kavadias*, first published by Hakkert, Amsterdam, 1987, and reprinted by Cosmos Books in 2007. He is included in a number of anthologies of modern Greek poetry, but is still, I believe, too little known beyond the borders of Greece. The late Jon Stallworthy, a brilliant poet, critic, and translator himself, was an enthusiastic reader and invaluable editor of my translations of Kavadias. He shared my opinion that Kavadias was among the greatest poets of modern Greece. Jenia Kavadias, the poet's sister, was my guide and companion on the long voyage I took with her brother's poems. Henry Kahane's *The Lingua Franca in the Levant: Turkish Nautical Terms of Italian and Greek Origin* (Urbana, 1958) was a trusty companion.

Iakovos Kambanellis' work, like Kavadias's, deserves to be better known. In Greece, he is best known as a playwright – some would say *the* playwright of twentieth century. He was a prolific dramatist, producing a play almost every year from 1950 to 1988. He was also a screenwriter, and wrote the lyrics for a number of Theodorakis's best-known songs. Interned in Mauthausen Concentration Camp from the beginning of 1943 until 1945, he published a single novel/memoir about his experiences entitled *Mauthausen*. My translation of his book was published by Kedros in 1995. Several of Kambanellis's plays have been translated into English including *Ibsenland*, and *The Four Legs of the Table*. A reading of Diana Savas's translation of the only other work that deals directly with his internment, *The Way*, was staged in Los Angeles in 2015.

Greek laments have been anthologized since the nineteenth century. In 1992, I published a book about laments: *Dangerous Voices: Women's Laments and Greek Literature* (Routledge, UK). In 2000, I published a second book about grief and mourning: *The Cue for Passion: Grief and its Political Uses*, Harvard UP). Both books have a large bibliography about lament. Recordings of lament are, for obvious reasons, difficult to find. I was fortunate to record a lament singer from Epirus, and others from Ta Ktismata, in eastern Epirus, before I left Greece, and to have had access to the field recordings made by Professor Sotiris Tsianis in Arkadia in the 1950's. Mariza did not sing laments, but she knew women in Mani who still performed them.

Mariza Koch has a large and varied discography. Starting in 1971 with *Arabas*, a sort of folk-rock album that became the first gold record in Greece, she recorded a series of albums that featured her own songs and arrangements of folk songs from various parts of Greece. She used rock and jazz musicians combined with folk instruments on albums like *Μια στο καρφί και μια στο πέταλο* (*One on the Nail and One on the Horseshoe*) and varied them with traditional children's songs and island songs. Two of her recordings of folk songs *Αγαίο* (Aegean) and *Τα Παράλια* (Coastal Songs) are fine examples of the best of Greek island music. She never produced an album of all her settings of Kavadias but her 2003 recording *Φάτα Μοργάνα* (*Fata Morgana*) has examples of her lovely settings of his poems. In 1990 she produced an extraordinary album without words called *Οι δρόμοι του μικρού Αλέξανδρου* (*The Ways of Little Alexander*). Some, but not nearly enough of her songs can be heard on youtube.

Dionysis Savopoulos's music is widely available on the internet. Among his best recordings are the 1966 album *Φορτιγό* (Truck), *Μπάλλος* (Ballos, 1970), *Βρώμικο ψωμί* (*Dirty Bread,* 1972), *Δέκα χρόνια κομμάτια* (Ten Years' Worth of Pieces, 1975) and *Αρχαρνείς* (*The Acharnians* ... who came back from the dead, 1977). He played the host at the Greek party that formed the finale of the Athens Olympic Games.

Notes

page 5. Lafiria means "booty" or "loot".

page 208. Miklos Nyiszli, quoted in Michael Matsas, *The Illusion of Safety: The Story of the Greek Jews during the Second World War,* New York: Pella, 1997, 118.

page 274. Archer, Laird, *Balkan Journal,* 1944. NY, Norton, pp196-199

Photo credits

Page 11. Photo supplied by Ms Koch

Page 13. Photo by Mariza Koch

Page 36. Photo courtesy of the Theodorakis archive

Page 43. Photo courtesy of the Theodorakis archive

Page 56. Photo courtesy of the Theodorakis archive

Page 61. Personal collection of the author

Page 72. Photo used with permission of the Greek photographer in Gail Holst, Theodorakis: Myth and Politics in Modern Greek Music(Hakkert, Amsterdam, 1980)

Page 80. Photo from an article by Frans Van Hasselt in HP, Amsterdam

Page 82. Photo from an article by Frans Van Hasselt in HP, Amsterdam

Page 89. Photo, Maggie Sadoway. Used with permission

Page 91. Photo by Eugene Vanderpoole and reproduced with permission

Page 92. Photo courtesy of the Theodorakis archive

Page 101. Photo by Eugene Vanderpoole and reproduced with permission

Page 109. Personal collection of the author

Page 131. Photo by Eugene Vanderpoole and reproduced with permission.

Page 133. Personal collection of the author

Page 135. Photo by Eugene Vanderpoole and reproduced with permission.

Page 139. Photo from Jenia Kavodias personal archive

Page 221. Image supplied by Katerina Anghelaki-Rooke

Page 249. Argyropoulos Photo Press
Page 250. Argyropoulos Photo Press
Page 252. Argyropoulos Photo Press
Page 255. Argyropoulos Photo Press

Fomite

A fomite is a medium capable of transmitting infectious organisms from one individual to another.

"The activity of art is based on the capacity of people to be infected by the feelings of others." Tolstoy, *What Is Art?*

Writing a review on Amazon, Good Reads, Shelfari, Library Thing or other social media sites for readers will help the progress of independent publishing. To submit a review, go to the book page on any of the sites and follow the links for reviews. Books from independent presses rely on reader to reader communications.

For more information or to order any of our books, visit
http://www.fomitepress.com/FOMITE/Our_Books.html

Nothing Beside Remains
Jaysinh Birjépatil

The Way None
of This Happened
Mike Breiner

Summer on the
Cold War Planet
Paula Closson Buck

Foreign Tales of
Exemplum and Woe
J. C. Ellefson

Free Fall/Caída libre
Tina Escaja

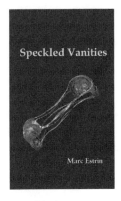

Speckled Vanities
Marc Estrin

Fomite

Off to the Next Wherever
John Michael Flynn

Derail This Train Wreck
Daniel Forbes

Semitones
Derek Furr

Where There Are Two or More
Elizabeth Genovise

The Three Lives of Jonathan Force
Richard Hawley

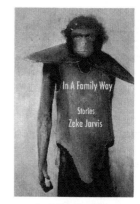

In A Family Way
Zeke Jarvis

A Rising Tide of People Swept Away
Scott Archer Jones

A Free, Unsullied Land
Maggie Kast

Shadowboxing With Bukowski
Darrell Kastin

Fomite

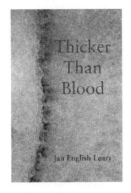

A Guide
to the Western Slopes
Roger Lebovitz

Feminist on Fire
Coleen Kearon

Thicker Than Blood
Jan English Leary

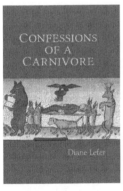

Confessions of a Carnivore
Diane Lefer

Unborn Children of
America
Michele Markarian

Shirtwaist Story
Delia Bell Robinson

Isles of the Blind
Robert Rosenberg

What We Do For Love
Ron Savage

Bread & Sentences
Peter Schumann

Fomite

*Planet Kasper
Voume 2*
Peter Schumann

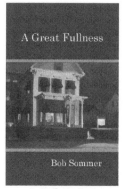

A Great Fullness
Bob Sommer

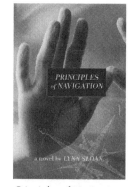

Principles of Navigation
Lynn Sloan

Industrial Oz
Scott T. Starbuck

Among Angelic Orders
Susan Thoma

*The Inconveniece
of the Wings*
Silas Dent Zobal

Fomite

More Titles from Fomite...

Joshua Amses — *Raven or Crow*

J Joshua Amses — Raven or Crow

Joshua Amses — The Moment Before an Injury

Jaysinh Birjepatel — The Good Muslim of Jackson Heights

Antonello Borra — Alfabestiario

Antonello Borra — AlphaBetaBestiaro

Jay Boyer — Flight

David Brizer — Victor Rand

David Cavanagh — Cycling in Plato's Cave

Dan Chodorkoff — Loisada

Michael Cocchiarale — Still Time

James Connolly — Picking Up the Bodies

Greg Delanty — Loosestrife

Catherine Zobal Dent — Unfinished Stories of Girls

Mason Drukman — Drawing on Life

Zdravka Evtimova —Carts and other stories

Zdravka Evtimova — Sinfonia Bulgarica

Anna Faktorovich — Improvisational Arguments

Derek Furr — Suite for Three Voices

Stephen Goldberg — Screwed and other plays

Barry Goldensohn — The Hundred Yard Dash Man

Barry Goldensohn The Listener Aspires to the Condition of Music

R. L. Green When You Remember Deir Yassin

Greg Guma — Dons of Time

Andrei Guriuanu — Body of Work

Ron Jacobs — All the Sinners Saints

Fomite

Ron Jacobs — Short Order Frame Up

Ron Jacobs — The Co-conspirator's Tale

Kate MaGill — Roadworthy Creature, Roadworthy Craft

Tony Magistrale — Entanglements

Gary Miller — Museum of the Americas

Ilan Mochari — Zinsky the Obscure

Jennifer Anne Moses — Visiting Hours

Sherry Olson —Four-Way Stop

Andy Potok — My Father's Keeper

Janice Miller Potter — Meanwell

Jack Pulaski — Love's Labours

Charles Rafferty — Saturday Night at Magellan's

Joseph D. Reich — The Hole That Runs Through Utopia

Joseph D. Reich — The Housing Market

Joseph D. Reich — The Derivation of Cowboys and Indians

Kathryn Roberts — Companion Plants

David Schein — My Murder and other local news

Peter Schumann — Planet Kasper, Volume Two

Fred Skolnik — Rafi's Tale

Lynn Sloan — Principles of Navigation

L.E. Smith — The Consequence of Gesture

L.E. Smith — Views Cost Extra

L.E. Smith — Travers' Inferno

Susan Thomas — The Empty Notebook Interrogates Itself

Tom Walker — Signed Confessions

Sharon Webster — Everyone Lives Here

Susan V. Weiss —My God, What Have We Done?

Tony Whedon — The Tres Riches Heures